GET ME OFF, ROD

True Stories of Lust, Lies, and Legal Drama

This book is a work of non-fiction based on true events. Some names and identifying details may have been changed to protect privacy.

For permissions, contact:
law@hylton-potts.com

ISBN: 978-1-0682311-0-0

First edition: 2025

Contents

Foreword 5
The Happy Ending 7
Caught Short 49
Miss Tan 78
You Are A Good Fuck 83
Just A Domestic 86
The Man In The Pink Suit 92
From Hero To Zero 107
Vote For Rodders 134
Goosing 161
The Human Lie Detector 170
That's Life 174
Unlike You, He Is 20! 177
White Van Woman 185
From Zero To Hero 190
Divorce Wars 200
The Diplomat And The Panties 218
A Prison Survival Guide 222
Had He Not Been Black 230
A Fisherman's Friend 232
We Don't Want Your Sort Around Here 235
The Vanessa Sex Letter 236
The Peking/Paris Rally & The Angry Ex-Husband 238
The Murderer And The Leather Jacket 241
The Portsmouth Penis Basher 243

The Doctor And The Soaps	245
The Case Of The Muffled Microphone	249
The Dentist And The Panties	252
Short Stories	256
Sling Your Hook	273
He Likes Big Horses	280
Fighting For Fathers	288
Refusing A Blow Job	292
Flo From Blow	296
In Closing	299
About The Author	301
Appendices	302

Foreword

For My Maudie

These stories are about some of the amusing and sometimes ground-breaking cases I have handled as a lawyer over the last 55 years. The bits about me are only to put them in context.

I am still not clear what presumption overcame me in writing this book, but maybe to make others believe they may profit from the squalid catalogue of my mistakes. The narrative is absolutely accurate, verified and fact-checked through my files. I have avoided any embellishment or exaggeration, which I hope will demonstrate that fact is indeed stranger than fiction.

However, as far as I have managed to carve out any fun and insight for the reader, huge credit must go to my wife and legal partner, Maud Bergvelt. She features on many pages, and I hope her skill, imagination and sense of fun emerge from the pages. My daughters Silvie and Stephanie were brilliant at spotting many mistakes.

All names are fictional unless stated otherwise. I have used real names for the cases that appeared in the newspapers while not breaching any confidentiality. I hope you enjoy reading the stories, and I hope that, like Maud and me, you will learn to never, never, never give in.

Rodney Hylton-Potts

The Happy Ending

"*I need to see you immediately.*" The voice was deep and powerful. It was the voice of an Alpha Male, somebody used to getting his own way in the boardroom and the bedroom. He had just a slight, cultured American accent; upper-class Americans do not speak in the whine that is often heard on US TV shows, such as Fox News.

The call came at 5:00 pm on 2nd April, 2009. My wife, Maud, and I were going on an Easter holiday to Africa at the crack of dawn the next morning, and this was the last thing I wanted. Still intrigued by the way the man spoke, I agreed to see him. He said he could get to my office, which was in our house in Fulham, west London, within 30 minutes. Before long, I heard the deep throb of an Aston Martin outside.

Our new client had quite a story to tell. His name was Donald - yes, as in Donald Trump.

His Tale Of Woe

He told me he was 50 and a wealthy hedge fund investor manager with a major problem that his regular legal advisers had totally failed to solve. In July 2006, almost three years prior, he had relocated from London to Monaco for tax reasons. His wife and daughter stayed behind in London, and he would visit them some weekends. Monaco is the most glamorous and low-taxation centre in the world. It attracts the moneyed classes and A-listers by offering zero income tax, a great climate, chic restaurants and boutiques, some of the world's best hotels and clubs, and beautiful people. The Royal Princes, William and Harry, made Vilebrequin swimwear the height of fashion, with the brand spotted at every hotel swimming pool in Monaco. It is also called ‘a sunny place for shady people’.

Donald enjoyed massages. One day, he saw a pretty masseuse wheeling a massage table as she was leaving his hotel and asked her if she did a mobile massage. She did. She was called Bella, which means beautiful, and she was a sexy, stunning brunette. She stood about 5 foot 4 inches, had light brown hair and hazel eyes, and was aged about 40. He told me he enjoyed saying her name, 'Bella', and that he told her so. The flirting had begun.

She began giving him massages at his apartment and, later, at hers, seeing him about once a week. She soon got the hint and, after that, there was a 'happy ending'. Donald usually took a shower and enjoyed a cold glass of white wine afterwards before going home to his apartment.

No harm done, no problem so far, and of course, not a word to the little wifey back at home. This went on for a few months. They had made love at his apartment overlooking the harbour and in her small flat on four or five occasions. He was having a ball, but he was getting careless. He told Bella about his family, his home and his work and took her into his confidence. That was something he would later realise, with the benefit of hindsight, was reckless.

Before Christmas 2007, he bought her a stainless steel Rolex watch. Then, he took his wife and daughter on holiday to Antigua in the

Caribbean, and from there, he sent Bella a postcard on which he wrote '*Bisous*' (French for 'kisses').

Donald Returns To Wifey

In March 2008, it was time to return to his wife and daughter in London, and he saw Bella for the last time. He gave her €20,000 in cash as a farewell present, with a card wishing her success in the beauty business she planned to start with the money. He would come to bitterly regret this deceit towards his wife.

Ten days later, having returned to his family in London (but had not yet wrapped up his affairs in Monaco), he was phoned on his mobile by a woman who said, in English, that she was called Fatima and was a friend of Bella, the masseuse. She had the distinctive accent of a black woman whose primary language was French. She demanded a meeting.

She said that Bella had been having an affair with her husband, which had cost her a good marriage, and that she had hired a private investigator to investigate Bella to get back at her and to get evidence for her to use in her divorce.

Fatima told him that the investigator had installed a camera and recording device in Bella's apartment and had recorded Donald having sex with her. She also knew about the 'Kiss' postcard from Antigua, the Rolex watch and the card he had given Bella with the money. She had a photograph of him coming out of Bella's shower. She rattled off his name, his wife's name, his address in Monaco, his address in London and even the fashionable London gym where he and his wife worked out. This was clearly a highly professional sting operation, and he knew he was in real trouble. He later learned that Fatima, a high-class prostitute, had gained access to Bella's computer without Bella's permission or knowledge.

Most terrifyingly, Fatima knew exactly where Donald and his family lived (in upmarket Mayfair in central London), the name and age of his daughter, the school she attended, and the name of the wine shop he owned. She threatened to turn up at his home and cause real trouble. She demanded €50,000 in cash in exchange for the photograph and notes, saying that otherwise, she would send them to his wife. She clearly had a mountain of private information about him, which she could not have found on the web.

He panicked, and his brain shut down. This is a normal reaction even for clever, experienced people. He did not go to the police. He certainly did not tell his wife. He consulted his regular lawyers, who told him he was stuffed but told him to play for time. They had no clue how to help him, but in fairness, as we will see, neither did I initially.

The Blackmail Plot

Two days after the phone call, Donald travelled to the south of France and met Fatima in a shop doorway in Nice. She was strikingly tall, very dark and looked about 35.

Fatima said she was from Nigeria and a 'working girl'. She wore dark glasses and a headscarf, with another scarf covering her face. Bizarrely, they shook hands. He recalled her hands were coarse, with hard skin. He had €50,000 in a briefcase in €50 notes. She insisted he open the briefcase to check for listening devices. She took half the cash and put it in her boots and the rest in a handbag.

He asked her to hand over the photograph and cards. She said she did not have them with her but promised to destroy them.

Donald was an astute and successful businessman and had been for years, so why on earth did he not demand the original photographs and cards in exchange for the money? That would be the obvious thing to do in such a transaction, but Donald panicked. His rational mind stayed shut down, and he felt like a rabbit in the headlights. So he let Fatima get away without handing over the photographs and cards and yet handed over money. He just hoped upon hope that it would all go away.

Fatima had promised this would be a one-off payment, but surprise, surprise, she came back for more. She was back in touch within days. She said she had had more expenses over her marriage and needed to pay her lawyers. More bullshit reasons. He knew that, but he was desperate.

At a second meeting, also in the south of France, he handed over a further €25,000, again with Fatima disguised with a hat, scarf and dark glasses. Once more, Donald failed to demand the original photographs and notes in exchange for the money. After this second meeting, he returned to live with his wife and daughter and to work in London permanently. Fatima had promised faithfully that she would demand no more money and that she had thrown away the photograph and cards. That promise lasted about five minutes.

More Money Demands

From April 2008, Fatima phoned Donald continuously on his mobile, demanding more money. He changed his mobile number, but Fatima called his office and his car phone. He told his secretary he would not speak to her, but Fatima then phoned his wife at home, pretending to be someone who had been sitting next to Donald on a plane. She explained to his wife that he had been very friendly and had asked her to get in touch. When Donald got home that night, his wife told him about the call. He could feel the blood draining from his face, but he believed he got away with it by saying he did not remember meeting anyone like that, but maybe he had. Donald's wife seemed happy enough, but experience shows that women have a sixth sense for these things, and Donald's dread of exposure and his panic just got worse.

Donald continued to make payments. He gave her his new mobile number to stop her from phoning his office or, worse, his home. Meetings between Donald and Fatima followed in Paris and Milan. He could not think straight. He was frozen in terror and getting into a deeper and deeper hole.

In May 2008, Fatima sent Donald a text saying she had sent a packet of 'evidence' to his old apartment in Monaco. Donald phoned her to say he was no longer there, and she became very agitated, hearing he had not been there to receive it. He agreed to return to Monaco to pick up the parcel from his old concierge and to make a 'final' payment of €20,000 to Fatima at a meeting in Nice, a few kilometres down the Côte d'Azur.

Fatima's next story was to claim that she had asked the investigators to break into her friend Bella's flat to collect and destroy the remaining evidence against Donald. She was doing this as a favour to him. She told him that the investigators had done so but were now demanding extortionate payments from her. She said Donald had to pay for this because of the favour she had done him. Donald wanted to believe this utter nonsense, which even Ian Fleming would not dignify with a paragraph in his most outlandish James Bond story. He desperately wanted it to be true, so again, he went along with it.

In July 2008, he travelled back to Monaco and collected the envelope from the concierge at his old flat. His mouth went dry, and his heart raced as he opened it. In it were photocopies of a photograph of Donald in a bathrobe at Bella's flat, a photocopy of the postcard from Antigua and the note with best wishes for Bella's new business. There was also a photo of the Rolex watch and a handwritten note from Fatima to say she had more evidence. The note was poorly written, as if by a child. With mind-blowing stupidity, again in a panic, Donald did not keep this handwritten blackmail note from Fatima. It would have been the first concrete evidence of her blackmailing him. He had never thought to record their calls or have her followed after their meetings. His comfort zone was Hedge Funds, financial markets, boardrooms and discreet meetings in London and New York clubs, not lurking in dark doorways in France and Monaco with a prostitute.

They met again. She had demanded, and he had brought €20,000 in cash as a 'final' payment. When he handed over the money, she demanded an extra €2,000, saying she had incurred further expenses. He walked with her to a cash machine and drew that amount out, but even that did not satisfy her. She insisted that he buy her some jewellery with a credit card because she had had to sell hers to pay the investigator. He refused, but eventually, they agreed that she would take his watch, an expensive Patek Philippe and that she would sell it. He gave her the watch, then went directly to Nice Airport and travelled back home to London.

Just imagine the scene. An experienced, intelligent, multi-millionaire businessman being bamboozled and manipulated by an uneducated prostitute. Do not be too hard on Donald. People behave that way in real life. We are not all James Bond or Albert Einstein. If we were, I would not have much business.

Subsequently, various texts were exchanged in which Fatima first claimed she had sold the watch but later said she had not, as she had become attached to it. She then said it was too unusual to sell and, therefore, agreed to return it to Donald, which, to his surprise, she did. It was delivered to his London offices by Chronopost, the French equivalent of FedEx. Crucially, an address and phone number were on the back of the parcel, which would prove crucial later when we were trying to track down this blackmailer. Donald had just got his first break.

The demands continued. Each time an amount was agreed upon, some drama would increase it. Inevitably, some form of disaster or unforeseen problem would emerge, further increasing the costs. It might be a missed airline flight, an insurance premium, a sick relative or a rental charge. She had a huge range of excuses, all of which he naively hoped were true and not just more extortion. She told Donald that the investigators had the disk with all the incriminating evidence on it, were demanding €50,000 for it, and again, she needed that money from Donald so that she could retrieve it for him. He got in deeper and deeper, feeling hopelessly trapped. He felt outwitted by Fatima, who was devious, slippery and clever.

Her next demand was to be paid by way of Western Union. Donald had little idea how this worked but discovered that cash could be paid into a branch in England and then picked up in a Western Union branch abroad, in this case, France.

Western Union payments followed - seventeen in all. In November 2008, Fatima said she wanted to fly home to Lagos, Nigeria, but had no money. She said she had no plans to return. Donald eagerly paid her the cost of a one-way ticket, hoping that this would be the end of it, but she never caught the flight and kept the money. Her demands were unceasing. Donald was at the end of his tether.

I Come On The Scene

Before Donald approached me in April 2009, he had already paid Fatima €263,000. Yes. You read that right. €263,000. He had met her several times to hand over cash or sent money via Western Union to the various names Fatima provided. Each time, it was a *'final payment, and then I will leave you alone',* but like all blackmailers, once she had got her teeth into him, she would not let go. In blackmail cases, the act of paying the money increases the hold the blackmailer has over the person and becomes one more obstacle to explain away. In this case, to a wife and daughter. Fatima planned to bleed him dry.

His regular solicitors could find no solution, so he had come to me. Could I help? I said I would need a retainer, and he paid by credit card.

He told me the prostitute Fatima was phoning and texting him daily, demanding more money. At our first meeting, I asked Donald to call her in front of me. He switched on the speaker on his mobile phone, and I recorded the call.

This is a transcript of the call. Bear with me. It's boring, but it will give you the flavour. And look out for the word 'pregnant'.

Blackmail Recording
Client and FB (Fatima)
2nd April 2009 6.45 pm
Listened to by RHP

CLIENT: Fatima, hi, it's me.
FB: Hello
CLIENT: Hi, can you hear me?
FB: Yes, I hear you
CLIENT: Oh OK
FB: What you saying?

CLIENT: Well, I called you because I'm fed up of texting; we went through this text, we did the whole agreement only last week that you go, you then send me the news about that, you say you're pregnant, and you then call again to say you need more money so, Fatima it's not what we agreed. We agreed many times that you'd do certain things, that you were going to give me the disk, you were gonna finish this whole process...

FB: If you want the computer, OK,

CLIENT: OK- Fatima you said these disks which are of me and Bella, you said these disks, the disks that you said you had of me many times had me and Bella on them, and that you had destroyed them and then you tell me that you have them. I said come to Paris to get them, and you didn't have them.

FB: No no no.

CLIENT: Yeah, OK, so you want to get together and money. I am fed up many times, money, more and more, and when I say more, I can't believe you threatened me again. You get angry, aggressive with me, you send me nasty texts....

FB: You say you send a lawyer; I am not scared you know. I want you but I have to have, but you know, if I love you very, very much, I have big admiration for you, but I want. I know danger, I know.

CLIENT: I can understand what you are saying, we agreed for a long time, every single time you say that we did, it doesn't work, you want more money.

FB: I need more money OK.

CLIENT: Fatima, let me finish - once and for all finished. I know that. I want once and for all for final time come to agreement, you not to call me, not my car phone, not call my wife. I never want to you to call my wife.

FB: I called your wife, because you never called me back.

CLIENT: I want to find a solution. I'd much rather you take not 2,000 euros, but 20,000 euros; you will always have more problems, in your life you always have need for more money.

FB: I have problems, Porsche, now with you, I have to pay,...etc. I can make you problems... I wait for you pay, I wait for your call, after my baby is born, I will tell you have obligations for the law.

CLIENT: I understand all of that, but I don't want to continue to do this. If you need money, that is fine, but I don't want to go on.

FB: What I saying I want to finalise everything- this has come all the time, whatever you want to do.

CLIENT: I want no further contact in any form on any level, no calls to the office, everything, no email, I want my life to be fine. If I can get the money together 20,000 euros on Monday, but then it is finalised. I want you to say yes or no.

FB: OK. the disks, the computer....

CLIENT: Now you are willing to give it to me, or we destroy it together? The disks.

FB: Next Monday. Tomorrow is Friday, Monday you will send me the money?

CLIENT: Yes 4 days. I want to meet you with 20,000 euros, and we destroy the disks together.

FB: You want me to give you the disks?

CLIENT: Yes. Where do you want to meet?

FB: In Paris? How about the money?

CLIENT: Give it to your friend, like I did for your birthday.

FB: Thank you.

CLIENT: OK, yes, I understand. Make it very simple. Send it to the PO Box.

FB: When can you do that?

CLIENT: Monday, tomorrow.

FB: Monday, we meet in Paris.

CLIENT:12 o'clock I will tell you exactly. Train times. If Tuesday's better, I can do that as well.

FB: I don't want to go to Paris unless you confirm.

CLIENT: I confirm so you can make your travel arrangements.

FB: I want to know at what time I have my money, and I can have my travel and hotel paid back.

CLIENT: Am I hearing you clear? We meet in Paris, I'll give you 20,000 euros for a better life, you will give me disks and end of all the blackmail.

FB: I never blackmail you, you don't you understand, I love you.

CLIENT: So, you don't threaten me anymore if I don't give you any money.

FB: If you won't enjoy......anyway...

CLIENT: I will call you.

FB: You give me extra than the 20,000 euro?

CLIENT: On top of the 20,000 euros? In addition to 20,000 euros? Are you saying I have to pay more than the 20,000 I offered?

FB: No, I am saying... travel to Paris, I need to go to hotel.

CLIENT: What I am saying, I offer you the 20,000 euros and you want me to pay more again.

Are you saying is this on top of the extra I have to pay the hotel. Is it an extra? On top?

FB: OK, so 20,000 euros for us, the hotel, travel.

CLIENT: Listen to me: you are saying 20,000 euros must be paid, plus other travel, plus hotel? OK, I will text you tomorrow, OK?

FB: You are sending me the 20,000 euros now?

CLIENT: You know that is not possible today, it is 7 o'clock at night. I will let you know tomorrow what I can do. Will talk to you tomorrow.

Sorry reader, that was so long but that is how people speak in real life. Lots of *Umm's* and *Oh's.* We all think we sound like television newsreaders but, sadly, we do not.

She spoke in a deep African dialect, with a French accent, and sounded intimidating. Donald had spoken about getting more money to her, generally tried to keep her happy and promised to ring again. I got the picture. He had not recorded any of his earlier calls with her. This call was recorded well. We now had a significant piece of evidence for a later criminal blackmail charge.

The reader will note that Fatima had claimed to be pregnant, more of which later. I told Donald I would need time to think, and he went on his way. He seemed happy to have someone to share the burden with.

Why Choose Me?

So why had he come to me? Between 1970 and 1996, I was a well-known solicitor in central London, handling numerous high-profile cases. In 1996 disaster struck and I served over two years in prison following a mortgage fraud conviction. I met such disparate characters as Lord Brockett, who buried Ferraris in the grounds of his stately home and made an insurance claim for theft, the 'lovable' Ronnie Knight, the career villain, married to actress Barbara Windsor and gangster Reggie Kray, to whom I offered my autograph to his great amusement. And there was Michael Fagan, who broke into Buckingham Palace in 1982 and sat on the Queen's bed, calmly smoking a cigarette.

I would not recommend prison. I lost my marriage, contact with my children, my home, my savings, my professional standing and the career I loved. Still, I set out to make the best of it - regarding it rather like National Service. I reset my life and my priorities, kept mentally sharp, and got and stayed physically fit. In those 30 months, I learned more about life than I had in all my 50 previous years.

Upon my release from prison in 1999, I did something The Times described as "*rare, even unprecedented*": I started a legal consultancy business in direct competition with solicitors.

The work poured in. Some new clients sought me out, hoping I would be the 'bent' lawyer they were looking for, but they were disappointed. What people wanted was a fighter and somebody who would never give in and would never give up until a solution was found. Somebody gave me the nickname 'Rottweiler', and it has stuck to this day.

I never tried to hide what had happened to me, and word got out that I was showing extraordinary determination and single-mindedness to avoid disaster (prison or otherwise) befalling my clients, as it had for me. For most men, it is loss of liberty or not seeing their children after separation, which are their nightmares. In Donald's case, it was discovered by his wife, resulting in the loss of at least half of his £50 million fortune and likely the loss of custody of their daughter.

Brainstorming

So, how can we help Donald? I set off on the holiday for Africa with my Dutch wife, Maud, who is also my legal business partner and about whom you will hear much more shortly. We talked about the case for the duration of the flight, which was about six hours. I hope the other passengers did not listen too carefully!

The solution to Donald's problems, as you will soon discover, was easy, but I did not see it. Donald did not see it. His former solicitors did not see it. Maud did. Maud, with whom I have been since 1999, is an extraordinary woman. Although she has no formal legal training, she has run businesses, experienced a messy divorce, faced court battles and problems herself, and possesses shrewd common sense and insight that few can match. Her nickname is '*Mystic Maud'*.

It was May 2009. We were in the garden of our home in London, having returned from our African holiday, and we were chewing over how we could help Donald. Maud and I love long lunches. It was the weekend. The sun came out. I think it was on the second (maybe even third) bottle of Chablis that she came up with the solution. "*If the tart thought the wife knew, the game would be up*".

"*Of course,*" I replied, "*But the whole point is that the wife must never know.*"

"*Hear me out,*" said Maud. "*If the prostitute met the wife and the wife said she knew, then the game would be up, and that would be the end of it. But the prostitute has never met the wife, so what we need is for somebody to impersonate the wife. And that would be me.*"

"*But you do not even know what the wife looks like or anything about her. She could be black or mixed race,*" I said.

"*Well, let's find out,*" said Maud.

<u>The Wife</u>

Fortunately, the wife, Melissa, turned out to be a white American, like her husband. He described her as a typical East Coast WASP (White Anglo-Saxon Protestant) - very classy, gentle and softly spoken, with dark hair, beautifully dressed and slim. When I asked him how she spoke, Donald told me that she sounded a bit like Jackie Onassis. This was important because, remember, Fatima had phoned the family home and had actually spoken to the wife. Also, the wife could readily be seen on the web at charity functions with

Donald, so she really had to be impersonated very closely, well and carefully.

We met Donald at his swish Mayfair office and put our idea of someone impersonating the wife to him (I had to take the credit as the boss!). He said it was brilliant, but he could not trust anybody. If we went to an actress, he could then be blackmailed by her. He needed somebody who could not only impersonate his wife and be absolutely convincing but who would be totally trustworthy. I told him about Maud's plan to play the wife, and rightly, he loved it. The solution was staring us all in the face, but it took Maud to spot it and say it.

Preparations proceeded apace. Donald provided photographs of his wife and a copy of her passport photo. He said he could get the original passport later. I knew things were getting serious when a CD arrived for Maud called '*Jackie Kennedy's Tour of the White House*', which Maud began listening to over and over, mimicking her voice. Maud studied the wife's web presence, photos and texts. We had to proceed - on the basis of what Fatima and her associates had done. We were clearly up against a well-organised, professional criminal sting operation.

Donald was worth £50 million or more, and a divorce would cost him at least half that fortune. He said he was quite certain that if his wife found out, she would divorce him. There would be no question of a second chance.

He asked me what I thought. I said that many women would forgive a short affair or a happy ending, or endings with a masseuse, maybe even a bonk or two, but they would never forgive repeated infidelity and the spending of €263,000 of family money on a prostitute. Also, Donald, having sent his mistress a postcard when on holiday with his family, would do him no favours. He told me that in Virginia (where his wife was from), her white society circles do not allow 'black' people in, and she would be sickened and disgusted by the fact that Fatima was black. (I thought he was right - that his marriage was doomed if she found out.)

Some men thrive on the risk and danger of getting caught. Perhaps that is why Donald did it. Remember Sir Allan Green, Director of Public Prosecutions. In that role, he was responsible for the majority of prosecutions in England and Wales and dealt with the appeals of the IRA Guildford Four and Birmingham Six. In 1991, time and time again, the police in the pickup, red-light area of seedy Kings Cross in London warned him for kerb-crawling and told him to go home, but he always returned. He got himself arrested, cautioned by the police and had to resign. His wife committed suicide two years later.

Lord Jeffrey Archer spent 18 months in prison for perjury. His trouble started when he visited prostitutes and then lied about it in court, despite having the gorgeous and, as described by the trial judge, 'fragrant' Lady Archer in his bed. It was the danger that seemed to have turned him on.

Alpha males and prominent figures sometimes seek out sex, often in public places, for no other reason than the thrill of their risky behaviour. Perhaps that explains what I learned next.

A Twist In The Plot

Donald and Fatima had developed a peculiar bond. He wanted out but seemed to have become obsessed with her. She claimed to have feelings for him too. In December 2008, he received a text from her which read: *'I just want you to make love. I never ask that to a man in my life. It is a very crazy situation. I leave now if you want, we can take protection. If you want, I can prove you'*.

This story now takes an extraordinary turn. Whilst being fleeced by this woman (remember Donald had met her on three or four occasions to hand over cash and even the watch on his wrist), he succumbed to her advances when she came on to him and touched him in the hotel room he had booked for them so that he could hand over yet more money.

After she pocketed the money, she offered, and he accepted, a blow job from her. After the deed was done, Fatima left the room to go into the bathroom. Whilst she was in the bathroom, he could hear her making spitting noises.

Three months later, the story becomes ever more bizarre. In March 2009, Fatima sent Donald a text claiming to be 2 months and 16 days pregnant, an oddly precise period of time, but which tied in with the date of the most recent money drop in the hotel.
She told him that she had impregnated herself with the sperm she had held in her mouth and, later, secretly deposited it in a cup in the bathroom. She claimed to be pregnant with his child with the help of a Brazilian fertility doctor, using a turkey baster. The reader will recall that Fatima mentioned being pregnant during the recorded phone call in my office on the first day I met Donald.

The hole Donald had dug for himself was becoming deeper and deeper. With this latest development, he was sure that if his wife found out, not only would his marriage be well and truly over, but he would also be saddled with child support for eighteen years or more, and the tart would have a huge claim over him.

Logic and experience would have screamed at Donald that it was all more fabricated lies, but when the brain shuts down, all logic disappears, and experience counts for nothing. We see this all the time with our clients.

The baby news was the last straw, and this was when Donald realised things were getting totally out of control. Pending Maud's fiendish impersonation plan, he instructed me to deal with her in any legal way possible.

The French Police

In May 2009, I swung into action. I filed a complaint with the French police in Grasse, South of France, accusing Fatima of blackmail and 'demanding money with menaces', but they did not want to know. Nothing happened. They were even less interested than the English police would have been in helping a wealthy businessman buy his way out of trouble. The French police and legal system are notorious for favouring French nationals and doing little or nothing to help foreigners.

Bella Comes Back On The Scene

Just when Donald thought his problems could not get worse, in May 2009, he was telephoned by the manager of the hotel in Monaco where he had regularly dined, who told him that Bella had called him asking for Donald's number, which she claimed to have lost. It was her birthday, and she seemed resentful that Donald had not called her. He checked, and it was indeed her birthday, but contacting him was not 'the deal' when they ended their relationship and when he helped her set up her new beauty business. Things were getting very uncomfortable. Now he had to deal with blackmail from the prostitute, a potential new baby and embarrassment from a former mistress.

The Campaign To Dupe Fatima

We then had to set about meeting Fatima, the prostitute, to get her into a room to meet the 'wife' and be told in no uncertain terms by the 'wife' that she knew and that the game was up.

Donald gave me all of Fatima's contact details, and we agreed there would be no more contact between him and her and that I would take over from here. I sent her an email saying that I had been instructed and that we would be making a payment to a lawyer of her choice, but as an absolute final payment, in written legal agreement. We had, of course, no intention of paying her a single euro more.

The French Lawyer

Maud and I travelled to Nice to talk to a lawyer recommended by the local Law Society as being shrewd. He was called Philippe. I explained the problem in his offices and was surprised to see he was making no notes. At the end of the meeting, Philippe said he recommended that we meet someone who could help, but that it must be outside the office in the open air after he had made a phone call. I agreed. Maud, Philippe and I went out into an open square outside the office and sat at a café table on the pavement. We were joined by a man who only gave his name as Michel. He said he was a former French Foreign Legion and he had heard the blackmail story from Philippe.

He recommended that he and his team should find the girl, take her to the woods, tie her to a tree and pour petrol over her head. They would then leave her there and tell her bluntly that the next time, it would be done with a match. This was spiralling out of control.

I said neither my client nor I wanted anything to do with such a scheme, and what made them even think that I would go along with it? Philippe said, "*We read about you on the internet*", which rather shut me up.

Fatima's Mother

We still had to track down Fatima physically. We had her phone number and email address but did not know where she lived. We only knew it was somewhere in the Cannes area of the South of France.

I was able to track down Fatima's mother with the help of French private detectives. The detectives visited her mother, and she answered questions about her daughter and showed them documents. One document was a hospital file showing that Fatima was due to have an abortion in a hospital in Antibes, South of France, but she had cancelled it. The clinic had made a note stating that "*She (Fatima) wanted to keep the baby*".

Although we had only slim leads, we were able to gather some information about Fatima. The French private detectives were excellent. They were able to establish that Fatima's long-term partner and father of her three children lived in the South of France. They unearthed a newspaper report showing that he was currently in prison for his part in a heroin network and a related shooting. These people were not lightweights.

On 27th June 2009, I visited her mother on a run-down housing estate near Nice. It was scary going into the seedy block, not knowing if I would be cornered or intimidated by heavies or worse. I needed to record the meeting. I went into the flat, and disarmingly, she offered me a cup of tea. We got chatting, and she admired my new iPhone. I put it on the table so she could admire it. Maybe she wanted it as a present. After all, her daughter had got an expensive Patek Philippe watch.

I had the recording switch on. Bingo.

She said Fatima wanted one final payment of €290,000 and would sign a document in full and final settlement. By now, on my advice, Donald would not pay a single euro more. Still, I said that €175,000 was doable if Fatima promised to appoint a lawyer to witness her signature to the agreement. The mother insisted that Fatima was pregnant. In a later phone conversation with the mother, she increased the demand to €320,000, stating that this would buy Fatima a house and that she would move to live in Nigeria. When I asked if Fatima would undergo a DNA test to see if Donald was the father, the mother refused point blank to consider this. She shouted and blustered as these ignorant people often do.

I wrote a legal letter to the mother. I write very tough letters, and it got her attention. It said in part:

'We have reviewed the evidence and are quite satisfied that both you and your daughter have committed serious criminal offences of extortion and blackmail. These amount to criminal offences both in France under l'article 312-10 du Code Pénal and offences in the United Kingdom and elsewhere, under jurisdictions where there is no time limit on criminal proceedings.

You are personally criminally liable and attempted to extort a further €320,000 when we spoke to you in your apartment on 27th June 2009. We recorded the conversation, which has been made available to the police and the procurer.

A complaint has been lodged against both of you with the Procureur de la République Service,
Grasse Cédex, France.

Also, civil action is being taken against both of you, other members of your family and those other accomplices who received funds via Western Union to recover the money extorted from our client. Apart from the €263,000 you extorted from our client.

You are well aware that we have tried to find a solution satisfactory to all parties and again and again asked your daughter to provide evidence of her pregnancy, one way or the other. Our client's wife, who is aware of all the facts, advises our client to pursue the fullest possible criminal charges and the most vigorous civil action. Matters might be different if your daughter could demonstrate that she is, in fact, pregnant.

We repeat that it would be in your best interests and the best interests of your daughter if she telephoned us and listened rather than swearing, shouting, and continuing her now totally irrelevant threats of further blackmail'.

Fatima Takes The Bait

After this broadside, Fatima took the bait. I got an email from her which read, "*Me, I am ready to listen and time to finalise emergency for Donald* ". More phone calls followed, and I was able, with the help of a translator, to speak to both the mother and Fatima and record their threats. This was getting exciting because I now had hard evidence of the blackmail. If the child had been conceived on or around 1st March 2009, the date of birth would be around 1st December 2009. That date came and went, and no baby materialised. Exchanges continued.

The promise of further money persuaded Fatima to appoint a lawyer, and she chose one in Paris, so that was our next stop. I told Fatima that Donald would pay her lawyer a good fee on top of the final payment. I told Donald I was pleased that he got in so much trouble in places like the South of France, Monaco and Paris rather (say) than Huddersfield or Bolton, but he could only manage a strained smile.

The stage was set for the ultimate showdown. The plan was that the client, Donald, with his 'wife' (Maud) and I, would travel to Paris to meet with Fatima and her lawyer. The lawyer was seduced by the prospect of a juicy fee on top of a 'final' payment to the prostitute. We never had any intention of paying any more at all; on the contrary, we planned to get the 'wife' to confront Fatima, saying she knew everything and that the game was up.

Bella In Monaco

Before dealing with the main problem, however, we had to take care of Bella, the masseuse, who had become an unnecessary and worrying complication. We were also unsure of her real connection to Fatima and its implications.

Maud and I travelled to Monaco, where Bella still operated as a masseuse, and checked into the hotel where she worked. We took with us an expensive Cartier necklace that Maud had suggested Donald buy for Bella as a final parting gift. Before making contact with Bella, we went to the fashionable Hotel de Paris in Monaco for a drink. We had a vague idea of tracking down Fatima. Boris

Becker arrived for his reserved table in the window, so we knew that we were in pretty heady circles.

Before we left the hotel, and without consciously thinking about it, Maud slipped a small sharp knife from the hotel drawer into her handbag. We were by now convinced Fatima was not operating alone and that she was involved in a complex sting operation with pimps. We knew we must be dealing with a gang and were well out of our comfort zone. This is the only time that I can remember going '*tooled up*' when I went out for a drink with my wife.

Quite by chance, at the bar, I met an old client who asked me what we were doing in Monaco. I told him we were trying to track down a prostitute who was blackmailing a client. He said, "*Why not ask her? She is the Queen Bee and runs all the prostitutes in Monaco?*" He pointed out a well-painted and well-dressed lady holding court at a table. To Maud's horror, I went over to her, showed her a photo I had of Fatima in my pocket and asked her if she knew her. She said, "*Absolutely, I know her well, but I have not seen her for a while*". You get nowhere if you do not ask!

Maud and I met Bella the next day and had lunch with her. She was sweet and tearful and said she was in love with Donald, but realised she could not have him. She chain-smoked and exploded with grief when we gave her the necklace, but she was grateful and obviously a thoroughly nice girl. She was sorry that Donald had got into such a mess and that she had unwittingly played a part in this. At least that was one less thing to worry about, but now we had to move on to the real problem of the grasping and dangerous Fatima.

The Showdown

The fun started during rehearsals. We all had to keep in part, and Maud threw herself into her task with relish. She acquired some good costume jewellery, bought a mink coat on eBay, and made herself look and sound more and more like the wife she would be impersonating. There followed the purchase of a dark wig, which had to be cut in the wife's style, not at a hairdresser's salon but by our hairdresser, Tina, an old friend we knew well, at her home for maximum secrecy. See Maud before with me and after her transformation

Donald had told us that his wife was a Democrat, and Maud made me laugh by saying that would make it much more difficult to carry off. Maud is a staunch Republican by nature and later became a strong supporter of Donald Trump, even though she is not American. In 2015, when he was still a rank outsider, she backed him at nine to one to become President, and the winnings paid for a Caribbean holiday for our whole family. So he has a very fond place in her heart. She repeated this triumph in November 2023, when she ignored the polls and backed Trump to win a second term, which he did with all seven swing states.

The Showdown Meeting

A meeting with Fatima and her lawyer was arranged and would be held in his office in Paris. We were staying at the Ritz Hotel in Place Vendôme, famous for being the hotel where Princess Diana had her last meal before the fateful drive into the tunnel with Dodi Fayed.

We arrived by Eurostar from London. Maud went into the hotel at about 3 pm as a blonde in jeans and a jacket and came out as a brunette in a long, striped mink coat. Our room was not ready, so she changed in the temporary room they gave us, which turned out to be the Elton John Suite, an incredible place covered in gold fittings befitting Sir Elton. The concierge gave Maud a very odd 'knowing' look, suspecting she was on the game and winked at me knowingly.

Dressed in the mink coat and jewellery, Maud also had with her the wife's passport, which Donald had surreptitiously removed from the safe at his London home. The dénouement would come when we met with Fatima and her French lawyer.

Because we suspected that Fatima was not working alone and must be part of a gang, we had to assume we would be under surveillance by her pimp and accomplices. I insisted that everybody keep in their role and play their part. We met Donald upon his arrival at Gare du Nord railway station.

It was a dark, murky Friday afternoon and, understandably and instinctively, the client Donald took his 'wife's' arm to help her across the busy French street to catch a taxi to the lawyer's offices. Maud was in full roleplay mode. She pushed away his arm and 'snarled' at him, "*Don't you touch me, you disgusting beast. You allowed that black bitch to put her red lips around your cock. You spent family money buying her off. You bring me to Paris on this humiliating trip, and you have the gall to touch me. Get off me.*" At this point, I almost lost it completely but managed to stifle my laughter.

Readers. Try this roleplay at home! Hilarious.

Fatima's Lawyer's Office

We made our way to a run-down part of Paris and located the lawyer's office over a tatty-looking tattoo parlour.

We met up with a delightful French translator I had hired. We took great care with our choice. Happily, she proved discreet and helpful. She just loved the case. Maud, the 'wife', remained across the street in a café while the three of us went up to the lawyer's office. It was shabby. There were papers and dirty coffee cups everywhere, and the phone in reception did not ring once the whole time we waited.

We met the lawyer, a rather slimy Frenchman aged about 50, who told us that his client, Fatima, was in the next room. Both Donald and I were incredibly tense. We had built up to this dénouement for weeks, and now the moment of truth was here. There was everything to play for. We risked the lawyer calling the French police and exposing Maud carrying someone else's passport. We did not know the risks, but we did know that French police side with the French.

The lawyer was already contemplating his fee, 10,000 euros, but was in for a big surprise. He expected the drafting of an agreement and a quick fee. Wrong! I told him that the game was up and that my client's wife was aware of everything and was waiting across the street, ready to come up to his office to confront him and Fatima. He was stunned, expecting a pay-off for his client and the juicy fee for himself. He began to harangue, then plead. Talks went on, and it began to grow dark. He turned to Donald and said, "*Monsieur. We are against each other, but this is France. This is a poor area of Paris with ram-raiders, drug dealers, handbag snatchers and muggers. Sir, go to your wife. I will finish things off with Mr. Rodney.*" I then nearly slipped up by saying, "*She is a tough old girl; she will be fine*", which did not fit well with the delicate Democrat 'soft petal' picture we had painted and the lady Fatima had spoken to. Maud is a tough Dutch girl who is well able to look after herself in any circumstance.

Fatima's French Lawyer Cocks Up

All was well, however. The one crucial thing the French lawyer should have done for his client was to check that the wife really was there and check her ID. Maud was ready to come from over the road, and my nerves were at breaking point. The drama was intense, but he did not even want to meet her and just took our word for it. In doing this, he made a major blunder.

Whilst Donald went to see his 'wife' over the road, Fatima came in. She was extraordinarily tall, and when I shook her hand, it was rough and coarse. She was like Naomi Campbell in stature and had an unpleasant, gravelly voice, which I had heard on the phone. She demanded her money. I told her that we had more money than her, more influence than her and more power than her. She was not going to get any more money, the police were outside, and we wanted all our money back. With this, obviously angry and frightened, she shouted in French. I could not understand her, but her meaning was clear. She was threatening and aggressive but then ran off, and we never saw her again. I had a row with the lawyer because he wanted his fee, but we told him to whistle for it and went back to our room at the Ritz.

The translator came with us to our room, a lovely French girl, and I was so relieved and the adrenaline was pumping so much that, when changing for a drink later (in the Hemingway bar at 30 euros a pop), I stripped down to my boxer shorts before realising she was there.

It was a successful outcome. We had a very happy client, and it all stemmed from Maud's lateral thinking. A simple solution. If the prostitute thought the wife knew, the game would be up. I missed it. The client missed it. His previous lawyers missed it. Maud got it. You do not need a fancy qualification to come up with sensationally effective legal solutions.

And Donald still has his fortune and his unknowing real wife. They are happily married to this day, but Donald no longer has massages.

Caught Short

David was 28, good-looking, with dark hair and single. He lived alone in a flat in London. He liked thrills and had just been to Thorpe Park, a theme park in Surrey, with his younger brother. It was a fine spring afternoon in May 2011. They went on various hair-raising attractions, including Logger's Leap, the same ride made famous by Princess Diana with her two young princes. Who can forget her drenched hair and her winning laugh?

On the way back, Dave and his brother had lunch in a pub about two miles from his brother's house. David was driving and, being careful about the breathalyser, had only drunk two pints. He was keen on his physique and was taking a bodybuilding drug called Creatine (not to be confused with Ketamine), which is a supplement that feeds the body with protein all day. A side effect, however, is that it can create an overwhelming urge to pee, partly because it works best when a large amount of liquid is taken with it.

Caught Short

David drove back and dropped his brother off at home, and set off for his flat in the car. He found he needed to pee badly, so he pulled up to the kerb in a street next to a park. He was desperate to go. There was no time to ask anybody where the nearest public loos were. In court later, he graphically said it was either going behind a bush or pee in his pants.

(Looking around London and other big cities, it always amazes me there are so few places to go to the loo. Tens of thousands of people are on the streets every day. Where do they pee? There must be a pent-up river of urine somewhere. I read recently that Greater Manchester had only eight public lavatories for the whole city, and that was before they closed three due to cuts.)

But I digress, back to David. Locking the car, David went into the park and found a nearby dense bush near the railings. He looked left and right and, seeing it was all clear, he relieved himself. (Men do this all the time, behind a bush, perhaps during a round of golf, or on a country walk, and it is no big deal, but the biggest reason for indecent exposure convictions is urinating.)

Black Lives Matter

In June 2020, during the Black Lives Matter unrest, a guy from Essex came to London, got caught short and ended up in jail. He liked a pint, so he had 16 of them during the course of a Friday, and he drank well into the night. Last time I checked, that was not a crime. Having had little sleep after his boozy evening, he came to London on the Saturday morning with his friends, with a vague idea of protesting that statues should not be torn down.

It was no surprise that he got caught short. He peed next to (note next to not on) a memorial of a Police officer who had been killed. He had no idea it was a memorial, let alone one of such importance. He did so discreetly, peeing between metal railings and as best he could to avoid being seen, especially by women or children. In the current climate, however, he was hauled off to court and charged with outraging public decency.

The proper, proportionate sentencing tariff for the offence of indecent exposure when urinating is a caution, but he got two weeks in jail and was branded by the Daily Mail **before** his trial as '*A racist thug*'.

I mention this to show that there are many different approaches to men who urinate outside. Whatever you think of David as the story unfolds, one thing is for sure: all he did to start with was have a pee in a bush in a park, having got caught short.

Sensibly, he wanted to get it over with quickly. He finished peeing, pushed himself back into his trousers and did up the zip. In his haste, however, he caught his penis in the zip, and it was excruciatingly painful. He undid the zip to free himself and then, more slowly, completely zipped up his jeans and walked rather gingerly back to his car. He sat in the car and, before driving off, decided to inspect the damage. Unzipping himself again, he took out his penis to examine it. He rubbed where it was hurting to ease the pain. He looked at his penis to determine if he had to go to see a doctor or had drawn blood. There was some blood. After the inspection, he put his penis back in his trousers and did up the zip on his jeans, rather more carefully this time.

The American Jogger In Her Pink Top

At that very moment, an American lady jogger in a pink top and black leggings jogged by with headphones on, running to music. She later told the police and the jury that she had caught David masturbating and looking at her in a seedy way, with his penis out, as she jogged past. She had not seen his face, but her attention had been drawn to his groin area. She jogged on a few yards but then stopped and memorised the number plate of his car.

The Arrest

Ten days later, David was at home enjoying his breakfast when there was a bang on the door. It was the police, mob-handed. They asked if he was the owner of the vehicle, and he readily agreed and invited them in. He thought it was a motoring offence. He was then told that they had reports of him indecently exposing himself to a member of the public. At first, he thought it must be a joke or a prank from his mates or his brother, but it quickly proved to be deadly serious. He was handcuffed and taken away in a Police car. The neighbours' curtains must have been twitching.

The police just love doing this. They often tip off the press. In nearly every case like this, it would be perfectly satisfactory to contact the suspect by phone, email or text to make an appointment to come into the Police station, usually with a lawyer. But no. Nothing is more exciting to a bored but overworked policeman than to have a dawn raid and a 'perp walk'. If the press could be tipped off in exchange for £50 in an envelope in the pub, so much the better. (Just ask Christopher Jefferies, whose arrest was all over the press. He was pilloried when a girl went missing because he supposedly looked like a stereotypical paedophile, with balding, floppy hair and effeminate boy scout looks. Christopher rightly received £500,000 in damages.)

The case proceeded to court. David faced an incredibly stressful, expensive and distressing ordeal.

Court

In court, our lady jogger explained that David was looking straight at her and was vigorously masturbating, leaving her shocked and disgusted. She gave a demonstration, moving her hand up and down and then round and round. In cross-examination, he said she could not see if he had tears in his eyes, nor could she see if he seemed to be enjoying what he was doing.

I Come On The Scene

David came to see me with his mother and explained what had happened. I said that I completely understood and we would fight the case. He then went to get his car to drive home whilst his mother waited. She asked me whether I could get her son off and whether I thought he was guilty. I explained that what I thought did not matter in the least. I did not tell her that I rather like defending people who are guilty because they are more grateful and often pay more. I hope this is not a shock to the reader. If you are in trouble, a lawyer is not your friend. They are your lawyer and can do more to help you than your friends can. If you want a friend, get a dog. And the lawyer does it for money. When people come to me in trouble, they are totally focused on getting off, hence '*Get me off, Rod*'. They are not interested in 'dinner party' talk about being guilty and getting people off or hypothetical situations. When you are in the hot seat and the shit has hit the fan, everything changes.

Does it matter if I think the client is guilty? Not in the least. Most clients are, but not all. I have advised a number of male teachers accused of fiddling with or touching children in their care inappropriately. As they tell me their stories, sometimes they get a thrill out of reliving it and put their hands in their pockets to play with themselves. Pretty disgusting. If that happens, they are guilty. David's hands remained in view.

David's Jeans

I told David's mother that what surprised me was that David had not brought his jeans to show me the blood on the zip to demonstrate what he said was true. I said I hoped the jeans had not been washed. I told her that if the jeans had not been washed, David should put them in a clear, sealed bag and get them to me by courier quickly so I could have them forensically analysed at a laboratory. She clearly had not discussed this with David. He arrived outside in the car, and his mother left.

Forensic Excitement

The following day, a courier arrived with a pair of jeans in a clear plastic bag, and I sent these off to a forensic expert for testing. The idea was that if there were anything on the zip, it would be subject to DNA and prove it was his after catching his penis in the zip. Blood, skin or hair would all tell a tale. They were blue denim jeans, and there were no obvious stains or marks in the zip area, the report concluded.

blood or skin that may have been deposited as a result of him catching his penis on the zip. Any material found could then be subjected to DNA analysis if necessary.

EXAMINATION OF ITEM

5.1 On the 29th of June 2011 I undertook an examination of the trousers provided by solicitors. This was a pair of blue denim jeans. No obvious body fluid stains were present on the zip area. The button at the top of the zip had apparent red/ brown marks or stains on it, but upon chemical testing this was shown to be some substance other than blood. It is possible that the marks on the button were as a result of wear or corrosion. No blood stains or skin fragments were located on the zip or on the area around the zip. The inner and outer surfaces of the zip area were searched.

5.2 Although blood stains or skin fragments were not detected on the zip, this does not mean that extremely small fragments of skin or blood stains were not present. It is possible that extremely small traces were present on the zip, that were too small to be seen with the low power microscope used by in the examination of this item, but given that the trousers were worn by, it would not be evidentially significant if such minute traces were present. Similarly, a
had worn the trousers it would be expected that traces of his DNA may be present on the zip. In view of this, I do not recommend further testing of the trousers.

5.3 Given that my expectation of finding traces of blood or skin material on the zip would be extremely low if penis had been caught in the zip, in my opinion the absence of any blood or skin material on

The zip does not assist in evaluating whether or not had caught his penis in the zip of his trousers

Chemical testing was inconclusive. Although blood stains and skin fragments were not detected on the zip, that did not mean that extremely small fragments were not present. They were just too small to be seen. The report added that the chances of finding blood, hair or skin material on the zip would be quite low if the penis had been caught. The absence of blood or skin did not really help one way or another in deciding whether he had caught his penis in the zip. An inconclusive report was disappointing. Juries place huge faith in forensic evidence, which sways their verdicts when witnesses say different things.

I reported the results to my client and his mother, and I could hear an audible groan from David. He found the inconclusive result of the report a massive disappointment. Later in court, in cross-examination, he was asked if he had ever grazed his knees. He replied yes, and was then asked if he had ever rubbed the graze, as he claimed to have rubbed his penis on this occasion. He said no.

The Charge

The charge was one of David intentionally exposing his genitals with the intention that someone would see them, who would likely be alarmed and distressed.

There now follows a summary of the exciting, contested court hearing which took place on 23rd September 2011 at Isleworth Crown Court. David had pleaded 'Not Guilty'.

The Prosecution

The Prosecutor was a lady barrister sent by the Crown Prosecution Service. Prosecution barristers are not there to press for convictions. They are not there to 'win' as is the case in the USA. They are there to fairly present those facts that suggest that the accused is guilty. We have all heard Sir Kier Starmer talking about the small boats in the channel, boasting of '*taking down*' criminal gangs, when he headed the Crown Prosecution Service. This is utterly improper for a prosecutor. We are not in the USA.

Every case starts with the prosecution outlining the evidence to the jury. The Prosecutor summarised the case and produced a map of where the lady had been jogging and where she said she saw the fully exposed penis. David was arrested 10 days later. Upon his arrest, he said he had gone into the park to urinate and caught his penis in his zip. That was good because being consistent in a story tends to lead to being believed. A jury's common sense tells them that.

In the interview under caution with the police, which the reader will have seen many times on TV in police programmes, David said that he eased the pain by holding his penis. The Prosecutor said to the jury that it was a matter for them to decide whether David had intentionally exposed himself or whether the jogger had been mistaken.

The judge granted an application by the prosecution for the jogger to give evidence from behind a screen. This was not good news for the defence team. It rather suggested that the judge thought the accused was, at a minimum, not safe for women. Juries often take their lead from the judge. As you read the next section, put yourself in the place of the jury. Decide what verdict you would have given.

The Lady Jogger Gives Evidence

The jogger was a white lady aged about 30. She was well-spoken, with an American accent, and was clear and concise in giving her evidence. She did not get flustered. She said that on 15th May she had been running in the park.

She told the court that she had stopped running as she came out of the park gate and began to walk. She was listening to music on her headphones. She said it was quite sunny, clear and not too hot. Her music was not particularly loud.

She came out of the gate and turned left. There was a man in a parked car, staring out at her and looking through his car window. She said she walked towards the car. She first saw the man when she was about three car lengths away.

She said he was staring straight ahead, facing in her direction. When she walked past his car, she glanced in and noticed he was uncovered in his trouser area - then looked again and saw that he was playing with himself. Her walking was at a normal pace, and the car window was up. There was no obstacle to her looking into the groin area. She said she stopped and looked again, wondering what she had seen and then looked again to check. The jogger then demonstrated a male masturbating movement and said that he absolutely was making eye contact with her whilst playing with himself.

She demonstrated the motion, and her hand went up and down. She said it was a vigorous motion and that she was shocked and disgusted. She was certain the penis was erect. She looked away and went to walk off but stopped just after the car and looked around to see if there was anyone else around - especially children or a family. She memorised the number plate from the back of the car.

She remembered taking her headphones off and running to her home, saying the number plate over and over in her head. When she got home, she wrote the number plate down in her kitchen and called the police.

The Lady Jogger Is Cross-Examined

It was then the turn of David's barrister to cross-examine our lady jogger. Under questioning, she agreed that the area was shady. She could not recall how many cars had been parked on the road. She said she did not sweat that much and did not have sweat in her eyes.

When she first saw David, he had not given any indication that he wanted to be seen nor made any suggestive motions or met her eyes. She had been wearing a bright pink vest top and black jogging bottoms.

Her attention was drawn to his groin area. She agreed that if he had tears in his eyes, she would not have seen them. Up to that point, he had given no indication that he was enjoying what he was doing.

There was nothing in his facial expression. She just had two fleeting glimpses of his erect penis, maybe two or three seconds. She agreed that when she was standing behind the car memorising the number plate, he made no attempt to hide his face or drive off.

I am now going to take the reader right inside that courtroom and quote from the transcript of the questions that were actually asked and answered. Put yourselves in the position of the jury and make your own mind up about whether David was guilty.

These were the questions to the jogger from David's barrister:

Question: *Is it possible that what you saw was an injured man soothing an injured penis?*
Answer: *His vigorous movements suggested he was not soothing.*
Question: *How many strokes took place in the two or three seconds?*
Answer: *He continued stroking up and down. It was difficult to tell how many strokes.*
Possibly more than half a dozen... Maybe, just a guess.
David's turn:

After the lunch break, David entered the witness box and was asked questions first by his own barrister. He explained how he had been to Thorpe Park and dropped off his brother.

Question: *The Location where it is said you committed the offence is Lamas Park Gardens. Is that known to you?*
Answer: *No.*
Question: *Why did you not ask someone where the public toilets were?*
Answer: *I was desperate to urinate – too desperate – so much so there was no one I could ask where the public toilets were.*
Question: *You say you were desperate to urinate. Where did you go?*
Answer: *A dense bush with a wall around it. I checked before I went into the bush; there was no one around.*
Question: *What did you do then?*
Answer: *I went back to my car.*
Question: *How did you come to be so desperate?*
Answer: *It was either that or do it in my trousers. I went to the toilet in Thorpe Park, then later dropped my brother off in Ealing. I was desperate to urinate. I was taking a bodybuilding drug called Creatine, which makes you want to pee.*
Question: *What happened?*
Answer: *My zip was halfway done up.*
Question: *Why halfway?*

Answer: *I may have forgotten to do the zip all the way up. I caught myself; I got into my car and realised my zip was undone. It hurt so much I had stomach cramp and leg cramp.*

Question: *What did you do?*

Answer: *I eased my trousers up.*

Question: *Describe how you did it.*

Answer: *My penis was still concealed in my boxers. I rubbed over where it was hurting. This was first attempt to ease the pain but it did not work.*

Question: *What happened next?*

Answer: *I decided, as it was quite a painful injury, to check it to see if I had to go to the doctors in case I had drawn blood. If I had injured myself, I would have had to go to the doctor.*

Question: *Did you look down at the injury?*

Answer: *Yes.*

Question: *What did you see?*

Answer: *I could see a little bit of blood there - a bit of a graze but nothing wrong with it. After 5-6 seconds, I put it back in my trousers.*

Question: *The witness says you were masturbating.*

Answer: *She is mistaken.*

Question: *What did you do?*

Answer: *For 5-6 seconds I eased my penis with my hand. The pain had gone. I had to rub my leg for a little bit. I eased my leg and then drove went home.*

Question: *Did you notice anyone?*

Answer: *No, no one.*

Question: *Do you recall a bright pink top?*

Answer: *No. I drove home about 20 minutes away.*

Question: *Do you live alone?*

Answer: *No, I live with my family, mum, dad and wife.*

Question: *Were they present when you got home?*

Answer: *Yes.*

Question: *Did you speak to them?*

Answer: *I remember speaking to my wife. I went upstairs. Told my wife what happened. She laughed it off, and I forgot shortly after the whole situation.*

Question: *Ten days later, you were arrested at home at 8 am?*

Answer: *Correct.*

Question: *Can you think of anything you did from that time to try and assure yourself that you had not committed an offence?*

Answer: *I should on that day have given my jeans to a forensics place.*

Question: *You submitted clothing?*

Answer: *Yes.*

Question: *Did it include your boxers*?

Answer : *No.*

Question: *Did you masturbate in your car that afternoon?*

Answer : *No*

Question: *Did you intend anyone to see you?*

Answer: *No*

Question: *Did you want to see anyone?*

Answer: *No*

David Is Cross-Examined

The Prosecution barrister then cross-examined David. Let me take you right into that courtroom again.

Question: *Was this the first time you had caught your penis in your fly?*

Answer: *Correct.*

Question: *So you cut your penis?*

Answer: *Grazed it.*

Question: *Afterwards, you told your wife?*

Answer: *Yes.*

Question: *What did you say?*

Answer: *I told her I had cut my penis.*

Question: *So it was not a major news event in your life?*

Answer: *I was arrested for indecent exposure.*

Question: *At the Police interview, you said you were arrested for indecent exposure.*

Answer: *That was not what they said to me - they said I had been masturbating in the car.*

Question: *Did not the two get connected in your head?*

Answer: *I could not put a date and correct time to it.*

Question: *You go home, speak to your wife in the bedroom, show her the blood and a cut.*

Answer: *More or less.*

Question: *You did not tell the police - Oh, that was the day I told my wife all about it.*

Answer*: I should have done.*

Question*: Thorpe Park - were you there all day?*

Answer: *I finished at 3 pm.*

Question*: Dropped your brother off?*

Answer*: Yes, I had drunk a large amount of liquid as I had taken a bodybuilding drug called Creatine in the morning.*

Question: *What is Creatine?*

Answer*: It is a supplement drink. You take it in the morning and it feeds your body with protein in the day, but the urge to go to the toilet is overwhelming. There is a warning on the bottle to drink lots of water and stay hydrated.*

Question*: Creatine; it does that to everyone?*

Answer: *Yes.*

Question: *Ealing station - you know it well?*

Answer: *Yes. Ealing Broadway.*

Question: *You dropped your brother off - you could have parked and gone to the toilet at Ealing.*

Answer: *I did not think of that. After dropping my brother off, I realised I needed to go to the loo. I took a shortcut through the park, then was overwhelmed.*

Question: *I put it to you that that is nonsense.*

Answer: *If you think this is nonsense, it is over to you.*

Question: *Overwhelmed? Why not pull in on the nearest road?*

Answer: *Silly if I had gone in the middle of the road.*

Question: *You could have gone in the park. You could have gone through the railings.*

Answer: *I went in the park and discreetly went behind a bush.*

Question: *You did not think of going into a café or pub?*

Answer: *No.*

Question: *In parks, virtually everyone has public toilets.*

Answer: *I did not know that.*

Question: *How old are you?*

Answer: *26.*

Question: *How many parks have you been to in your life?*

Answer: *(No Reply)*

Question: *Why not go by the railings? Could not you stand and pee by a tree?*

Answer: *I did not think of standing against the railing.*

Question: *You come up with this incredulous story about needing the toilet.*

Answer: *That is incorrect.*

Question: *You did not need the toilet, did you?*

Answer: *I was desperate to urinate.*

Question: *You go to toilet -*

Answer: *I was wearing zip-fly jeans. I went to the toilet and put my penis back in my boxer shorts.*

Question: *No erection?*

Answer: *No.*

Question: *Sure?*

Answer: *Sure.*

Question: *You get in your car and see your flies are half undone.*

Answer: *Yes.*

Question: *You had caught the top of your penis?*

Answer: *Correct.*

Question: *Did you cry out?*

Answer: *I did.*

Question: *Then you say you put your hand over your groin.*

Answer: *I got my penis out.*

Question: *Why did you think it would help?*

Answer: *It was grazed.*

Question: *Have you ever grazed your knee as a child?*

Answer: *Yes.*

Question*: Did you rub your graze?*

Answer: *I cannot remember.*

Question: *No one can mistake masturbating vigorous strokes to your so-called soothing actions.*

(Prosecution counsel makes masturbating movements and compares with soothing movements.)

Answer: *She is mistaken.*

Question: *Did it rip your boxer shorts?*

Answer: *They got stuck with a bit of skin in my boxers.*

Question: *What did you do with the boxers? Was there blood on the flies?*

Answer: *No, only on the penis.*

Question: *The account you have just given us is that you cut and made your penis bleed, yet there was no blood on your boxers or trousers. All this in 5-10 seconds for the first time in your life, and it must have coincided with the woman walking by.*

Answer: *Incorrect.*

Question: *You say you rubbing the injury coincided with the woman walking past.*

Answer: *Yes. I was soothing the injury.*

Question: *You must have seen the woman in the bright pink top.*

Answer: *I never saw her.*

Question: *You get gratification from masturbating in a public area.*

Answer: *No. I do not.*

Question: *You had cramps in your leg. Stomach pain. But you did not go to a doctor because you did not injure yourself.*

Answer: *I did, but it did not bleed as much as I thought it would.*

Question: *You parked by the park to masturbate.*

Answer: *Incorrect.*

Question: *Your story is so you can get away with masturbating in a public place.*
Answer: *Incorrect.*

David left the witness box.

The Prosecutor Sums Up

After a break, prosecuting counsel summed up for the jury.

Members of the jury. You have got the gist. The choice is between two gestures that are so distinct that someone has lied and someone has not.

The accused gets gratification from masturbating in public, so he needs to come up with a reason why his hand is on his penis. He needs to come up with a story to convince you, so he naturally lies with the penis-in-fly story.

He likes masturbating in public places. It was a bright day. There was some shade, but the jogger was only a few feet away. She glances in his car window. Takes a second and sees him carry on. He must have seen the woman in bright pink. He carried on. He did not cover up his groin area. Why? He is enjoying it. Why not cover his penis, if it had been hurt?

The lady jogger said that no effort to cover it was made. There was nothing ambiguous about the movements she made - the keyword is 'vigorous'. She said he masturbated six times.
If his story had been true, he would have gone to see a doctor. She had no reason to make this up. She was nervous in court. She was uncomfortable with what she saw. It is a matter for you whether he pulled up by the park to masturbate. She saw him from a foot away in her bright pink top. You will be told by the judge that you must be sure. It was only for a few seconds, but she was sure. So can you be?

David's barrister then summed up for the jury:

Prosecution counsel told you at the start of the case that the burden of proving innocence or guilt is on the Crown. The accused does not have to prove he is innocent. The standard the Crown has to reach for that proof is a high one. It is beyond a reasonable doubt. If you have any doubts about any element you need to get a finding of guilt, you must acquit.

The accused is charged with the following offence:
Section 66-a person commits an offence if:
a) he intentionally exposes his genitals and

b) he intends that someone will see them and cause alarm and distress.

You need to find guilt in both those elements.

The evidence that we have is quite short - just the lady jogger called as an eyewitness for the Crown. It has never been disputed that the accused exposed his penis. The lady told us he caused her alarm and distress. She told us she had been jogging. She slowed to a walk. She did not see his car until she was 3-4 car lengths away, which is an average car length. She told us he was staring ahead at the time. She was on the pavement to the side - so he was not looking at someone on the pavement. She told the court there was something about what she first saw that made her uneasy.

You may think she made her version sound beefier in court than in reality. She got next to the window. She looked into the car. She looked at him for one second, not even five seconds. Which is how long he said he was rubbing his injured penis for. She did a double take. She said she did not look much longer. It was a fleeting glimpse, yet she said she saw a vigorous motion. Can you be sure he had not injured his penis and was soothing it?

She had never seen my client before. Can you be sure she was right that he was masturbating? The accused says he was not. You have to decide he was doing it deliberately.

The lady jogger says he never gave her any eye contact. He did not beckon. He never did anything with his eyes. She was quite sure. If he had been masturbating, with the intention that someone could see it, it was, as it were, a bright pink opportunity ***(forced laughter in court)****, an ideal opportunity.*

Surely, he would have done something to make sure she stayed watching him enjoying himself. It is clear he was oblivious to what was going on around him.

The prosecution says he was enjoying himself - but the police did not test his car for semen. They knew who the car belonged to and where it was kept, and by the time the detective was assigned, there would have been a good opportunity to go over to the car and have it tested. The Crown cannot say that whatever he was doing, he was getting sexual gratification from it - because there is no evidence of that.

That is the prosecution case at its highest. Have they proved to you that the accused intended to expose himself? The accused gave evidence. It was wholly consistent with the account he gave to the police. He did not try to beef up his account today. You may think he was a credible and honest witness. He was subjected to quick-fire questions from the prosecution, and he acquitted himself well. He has never been in trouble with the police before, on suspicion of exposure, or in trouble with the police at all. He is a credible witness. The lady tried to beef up her account today.

OK, reader. Decision time. You are on the jury. Would you convict or acquit? Are you sure David did it? Or do you have doubts?

The Verdict

He was found guilty and ordered to do community service. (I still think there are not enough public loos).

The Final Twist In The Tale

Remember the forensic examination that came back inconclusive? When the case was over, David told me the extra part of the story. Remember the forensic test we had done on the jeans? The blue jeans he had been wearing that day had been washed, so when he heard from his mother that it would help to send me his jeans for forensic examination, David had gone to his bedroom, put on another pair of blue jeans and deliberately zipped them up to catch his penis in his jeans - in effect mutilating himself, in the hope that the blood/skin/DNA would be attached to the zip, as I had suggested. This would have got him off.

Talk about a bad hair day!

Miss Tan

When Donald and David came to see me in my office, at my home in London, they and other clients were always impressed to see my beautifully bound, red law books. I hope they did not see the layers of dust on them, seeing as I rarely opened them, but they gave the appropriate air of gravitas and learning.

In my library, I had the famous yearly legal book, the All England Law Reports. These record important cases of how judges have interpreted statutes created by Parliament. They also set out basic rights given to us all, such as the right to silence and the presumption of innocence.

Most of these books were about an inch and a half thick, but just occasionally, a volume appeared which was at least twice as thick as the others, and I often wondered why. Eventually, I decided to investigate. I identified and pulled out the books that were fatter and found the reason.

In the Court of Appeal, whose decisions resulted in the bulk of the cases reported, there are three Judges who often give unanimous judgement, three/nil in football terms. Typically, the most senior judge sits in the middle of the three, reads out his judgment, and the two other judges will say, "*I agree with my brother*" or "*I agree with Her Ladyship*".

Occasionally, however, each judge reads out their judgement, reviewing the facts of the case in great detail and repeats them even though the senior judge has already done so. What were these cases? Without exception, I discovered they were cases of a sexual nature. One of the fattest volumes dealt with the case of *R v. Tan*. Miss Moira Tan (as her name suggests) found her popularity in tanning the backsides of her male clients. Indeed, so successful was she that she declined to offer any sexual services at all other than caning and spanking. Intercourse was out. She was the first known Miss Whiplash to appear in the Law Reports.

To complicate matters, she had started life as a man but was undergoing a sex change operation. The legal case turned on whether a person, born a man at birth but undergoing a sex change operation, could be a prostitute for this purpose, whether another man could live on their earnings, but more particularly, whether premises that offered no sexual intercourse were a brothel.

<u>The Clients</u>

The services offered by Miss Tan were very popular, and it was said, without naming names, that there were lawyers, judges, MPs, accountants, business leaders and even vicars queueing up to be tanned by Miss Tan, or rather Mr Tan if only they had known. It is accepted now that many Alpha males who run their own businesses or are otherwise successful in life crave pain and humiliation and the excitement of somebody else being in control.

In court, each judge (all male) found it necessary to go into the greatest detail of the case, particularly referring to the outrage of public decency and, condemning such behaviour and calling for punishment. It reminded me of the famous News of the World headline, "*We condemn the spanking vicar*", which then continued to condemn him roundly over eight pages!

The Lord Chief Justice explained that "*The services provided at the premises were of a particularly revolting and perverted kind. Straightforward sexual intercourse was not provided at all. With the aid of a mass of equipment, some manual (such as whips and chains), some mechanical and some electrical, clients were subjected, at their own wish and with their full consent, to a variety of forms of humiliation, flagellation, bondage and torture, accompanied often by masturbation.*" The judges reviewed, in minute detail, previous cases on female domination and mused aloud whether the premises could be a brothel if there was a large sign in neon lights over the door containing an open invitation to be whipped or subjected to any form of perversion, with a price list set out. The merits and popularity of each particular service and the prices seemed to interest the three male judges particularly.

The premises were advertised in contact magazines in the following way:

> *89b Warwick Way*
> *Humiliation enthusiast, my favourite pastime is humiliating and disciplining mature male submissives in strict bondage, lovely tan coloured mistress invites humble applicants ...*
>
> *15 Clarendon Street*
> *The most equipped mistress in town. Report now for corporal punishment, dungeon, TV wardrobe, stiletto heel boots, e-shocks, maid training, you name it, Madam has it...*

Such adverts can be found today all over the internet, but in 1983, they were considered by the judges to be, as they put it, particularly revolting and perverted, and prison sentences were dished out to the girls. These days, rightly, the police shrug and, I almost said, turn the other cheek.

So next time you visit your lawyer and see a law book on his bookshelf that is fatter than its neighbours, you will know why.
And of course, if, for purely academic reasons, you wish to study the case in detail, it is in the Appendix.

You Are A Good Fuck

Clive was a good, long-standing client. Divorced with grown-up children, he had little baggage and lots of girlfriends. He was darkly handsome, with a neatly trimmed beard.

Many of my male divorce clients grow a beard after separation from their wives. They must do it to appear more attractive. Anyway, it does not work! Most of them just looked dirty and older. Designer stubble is all the rage for those whose beard can be a bit straggly.

Clive had come to me with several legal problems over time. On this day, he brought his latest girlfriend to meet me. He said he had talked to a specialist defamation solicitor about the current problem but that he and his girlfriend wanted a different type of approach and a second opinion.

His girlfriend, Yasmin, was Iranian and looked about 30. She had long, shiny, dark brown hair and a dazzling smile. She wore fashionable jumpers and shining boots, very suited to a polo field. She was voluptuous, with bright red lipstick and wore a strong, heady perfume. She exuded sexuality. She spoke quickly and in poor English. Like many foreigners, she assumed that we Brits could follow.

Yasmin explained that she was a private nurse and had received a letter from a former boyfriend whom she had met at a hospital that she found very offensive. She said she had highlighted the offending parts with an orange highlighter pen, and indeed, she had. She handed over the letter as though it was a piece of dog excrement.

I read the letter, which was loving, even passionate, and not at all aggressive, but which included the immortal line, "*You are a good fuck*". I asked her why she was meeting me and what she wanted me to do about the letter.

She said, "*I want action.*" "*Do you?*" I said, teasing her, but this was not going well. She did not appreciate my humour. I have found that humour is a huge part of successfully handling clients, but some foreigners, especially Russians, never see the funny side. I became more formal.

I explained to her that there were two legal hurdles she had to overcome before any action could take place. The first one: did she find the letter offensive? "*Absolutely,*" she said. "*Very offensive.*"

And, if so, the second hurdle: was it true? In other words, was she a good fuck? Losing patience, she said, *"OK, Mr £1000 per hour. So what is your advice?"*

I told her: "*Take the letter home, frame it, hang it on the wall of your loo to show your friends, and thank heavens it does not say you were a bad fuck.*"

They both stormed out and refused to pay my fee, and I lost Clive as a client. But who cares; it was worth it to see her face. And to this day, I wonder: was she?

Just A Domestic

John was a top Consultant Orthopaedic Surgeon, aged 53, who specialised in rebuilding bodies after serious accidents. Having achieved a first-class degree at Oxford, he had a distinguished and successful career in orthopaedic surgery. His patients included celebrities, politicians and millionaires. He was tall and impressive, spoke beautifully, and his patients had huge confidence in him. He appeared to be on top of his game. Unfortunately, he held a dark secret. He was a serious, chronic alcoholic who loved living life on the edge.

He lived in a house in Chelsea, near the hospital where he worked. He drove a Mercedes convertible sports car with a personal number plate and enjoyed wearing expensive suits and going on elegant foreign holidays, usually in the Caribbean. With an income of £500,000 p.a. plus, he could afford them.

John's Secret

He drank a bottle of vodka every day, then self-medicated with Valium and tranquillisers before being able to function. After theatre, he would go home and start drinking again. His colleagues had no idea that he took beta-blockers before surgery to keep his hands steady after a heavy night.

Over the years, he had an excellent safety record, but latterly, there had been complications. One of his patients required an amputation after one of his operations; another had a wire left in her leg without adequate anaesthetic. Two more had died. The General Medical Council, which disciplines erring doctors, were getting interested in him. Legal letters from patients' lawyers had begun to arrive. His insurance company was getting edgy. In an all-too-typical downward spiral, his drinking became heavier.

Louise

He found solace in the arms of a girlfriend, Louise, a stunning black girl about half his age who lived in Notting Hill. The fun that brought John and my firm together started on a Saturday when he had no patients the following day. He had a date with Louise. As he drove up to her flat in his Mercedes to pick her up, she was leaving in a black cab, giving him the finger through the rear window. He was furious. He followed her cab and phoned her on his mobile. They spoke and she said their relationship was over, although in shorter words than that, mostly with words starting with a letter near the start of the alphabet.

Their relationship had had its ups and downs. When she broke up with him on an earlier occasion, he followed her disguised in a Russian fur hat and false beard. There was the ever-present hip flask of vodka in his jacket pocket.

Not satisfied with her brush-off and enraged with the finger, he continued to follow her cab and tracked her until she went into a nightclub. He drove back to Notting Hill, parked near her flat and found a pub. Further fired up by several vodkas, he decided to wait until she got back, but no clear plan formed (or if it did, none was retained in his befuddled brain).

Eventually, she arrived by black cab and went into her flat. I was never quite sure why he did not confront her in the street. Maybe he needed another vodka for Dutch courage. It was probably just as well he did not. He rang the bell repeatedly and banged hard on the door, but she didn't answer. She phoned the police, who said that they could not get there quickly. Saturday nights after the pubs shut are an incredibly busy time for the police. They advised her that she should record the ringing, knocking and anything he said on the phone if he phoned until they could get there. This proved to be good advice for her, but most unfortunate for him.

As she and the police expected, he phoned her mobile phone, furious that she would not let him in. He shouted into the phone, "*Go back to Africa where you came from and swing from the trees*". Louise's phone recorded that very clearly. With that, he kicked at the door, causing what later proved to be £248 of damage. The door was solid, held, and he went home. The police arrived at her flat the next morning, and she made a formal complaint, playing the recording on her smartphone. Later, John was arrested for criminal damage and aggravated racial harassment.

John In Deep Trouble

John could easily have afforded to pay the £248 repair charges, but what he could not afford was a criminal conviction of this type, or any type, as this would have ruined his career. The General Medical Counsel's Fitness to Practice and disciplinary hearings must be heard in public, by law, and the press would have had a field day. '***"Go back to Africa and swing from the trees," says Top Surgeon',*** would be the headline. It is a perfect story for the Daily Mail, Sun or Mirror. He would also have been struck off as a doctor. To add to his woes, he was getting phone calls from Louise's friends, demanding an odd amount, £27,000, with a promise to drop the case. On my advice, he managed to get some of this blackmail on tape, but this had the potential to turn very nasty indeed.

I was instructed on the recommendation of one of his former girlfriends. Ironically, later, this same girlfriend complained about his negligent treatment after he had operated on her, resulting in injuries causing her to have problems walking. My aim was to try to get the Crown Prosecution Service ('CPS') to drop the case. John had the money and resources, so we successfully applied for adjournment after adjournment. He had to go to Court eight times, but each time we managed to get the case put off. Someone on legal aid would have been convicted and sentenced long beforehand. John was not on legal aid.

One meeting with the CPS at their office at the Westminster Magistrates' Court was particularly useful. I was able to read some strategy notes on the prosecution file. I read them upside down. Yes, I have taught myself to read upside down. It is a very useful skill.

All this gave us breathing space to come up with a plan. We hoped to convince the CPS that it was really a 'domestic' and that they and the police had better things to do. They are very heavily engaged in chasing 1980s disc jockeys and white men for so-called hate speech. We handed the police a CD recording of the blackmail threats, but nothing much happened, and that did not convince the CPS to drop the case. It ground on and on.

A Twist To The Tale

Then, there was a dramatic development. Just before the ninth hearing, John went for a drive in his Mercedes. He drove off but almost immediately pulled up to the kerb and found that two of his tyres had been slashed. He was rightly worried for his life because he could have been killed and, therefore, on my advice, he told the police what had happened. They arrested his ex-girlfriend for attempted murder. She was quickly released due to lack of evidence, but the CPS then decided that this was, after all, a 'domestic' between two lovers and the case against John was dropped.

Who so conveniently slashed the tyres on John's car remains a complete mystery. I have my suspicions but could not possibly comment.

The one thing I will say is: never, never, never give up or give in!

Happy with the outcome, John became a client for further problems, which included an arrest for attempted murder of a prostitute in a bondage sex game gone wrong (which allegation was later dropped) and driving four times over the breathalyser limit. Sadly, he fell downstairs in his house and died about a year later. Alcohol literally proved to be the killer in his case.

The Man In The Pink Suit

My client, Dave West (his real name), was the salt of the earth.

Originally from Romford, Essex, Dave started his career working as a market trader boy. When he was 18, he joined the Merchant Navy. He built the family tobacco business in France and Belgium with his wife and children. Returning from a holiday in France, he had noticed how many of his fellow travellers were stocking up on wines and spirits from the local supermarkets before boarding the ferry home.

Making money for Dave had been surprisingly easy. His rags-to-considerable-riches rise from the family stall in Romford market was every barrow boy's dream. At 25, when probably destined to work the markets all his life, he had spotted a particular gap in the wider market.

In 1980, he started a wholesale business on a double-decker bus near the ferry terminal in Calais, selling cheap, duty-free alcohol and cigarettes. He called his business 'EastEnders', a name dreamed up by Kathy, his wife, who loved the TV soap. The business became the largest British cash and carry group in Europe. Dave also had his own house wine labels, '*The Dogs Bollocks*' and '*Ménage à Trois*'. He became a millionaire many times over.

Dave Hits The West End

Business was good, and Dave accumulated plenty of money, often in cash, but he was homesick and wanted to come back to England. Knowing nobody and being by then divorced, he decided to open a club as a base for his social life, opposite the fashionable Tramp Nightclub in Jermyn Street in central London. Tramp is famous for Prince Andrew not sweating there and not buying any drinks at the bar either, or certainly having no recollection of doing so. Maybe it was something he ate at the Pizza Express in Woking earlier that day. But then, of course, recollections may vary.

Dave was a flamboyant figure who attracted and loved publicity. He wore a bright pink suit with a pink top hat. When he attended the Royal Enclosure at Ascot as my guest, he arrived in a formal grey morning suit, changed in the loo into his pink suit and pink top hat, and handed out flyers for his Mayfair lap-dancing club '*Puss in Boots*' to our fellow racegoers. My wife and legal partner, Maud, was mortified. At lunch, he introduced his girlfriend, who got my attention by mentioning she was not wearing panties. Very classy.

Bondage Tables And Penis Taps

His nightclub was called HeyJo after one of his girlfriends, Jo, and the restaurant he also owned, Abracadabra, featured a private room with a dining table, which turned over to reveal bondage equipment. At each corner of the table was a strap to restrain wrists and ankles.

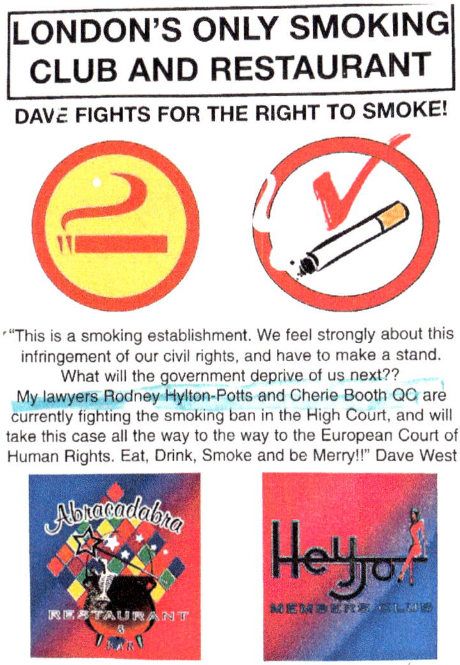

He saw and described himself as a libertarian and nonconformist. He was an active protester against the smoking ban. In August 2007, he hired me, and I briefed Cherie Blair QC in his bid to challenge the ban (introduced by her husband and Prime Minister at the time, Tony Blair). He insisted the ban was an infringement of his customers' rights to smoke in his club and restaurant.

Cherie visited the club and was intrigued by the penis-shaped gold taps in the ladies loo. When Dave explained that they were modelled on his, she looked sceptical. If they were, he was exceptionally well endowed. Dave, Cherie and I ended the tour on the steps of his club in Jermyn Street. Dave made sure a photographer was on hand.

The Other Essex Boy Made Good

The following year, Dave paid more than £100,000 to attend David and Victoria Beckham's charity World Cup Party and said that he was subject to such an unwelcoming pre-party briefing that he chose to boycott the event. After winning the bidding for the two tickets in an online auction, he was instructed to sign a confidentiality agreement, as well as being banned from handing out his business cards to guests or taking his mobile phone and camera to the party. He said: "*The confidentiality agreement would mean that had I signed it, I couldn't talk about the party, even to my friends.*" West insisted that such conditions were unheard of. Perhaps David Beckham had an eye on his knighthood. Just like Dave, he was an Essex boy made good. Maybe it was 'Posh Spice' being posh, or maybe it was because Dave had refused to sell his personal car number plate DAV1D to David Beckham, who offered him £350,000 for it.

Dave had successfully bid £103,000 in an online auction in aid of the NSPCC for two tickets to the ball, which was being held at the couple's home in Hertfordshire. It was a night that brought together Joan Collins, Wayne Rooney, the Duchess of York and a tieless Prime Minister David Cameron, who were amongst the 400 celebrity guests - but not Dave West and his then-girlfriend.

Dave claimed that he had received a call from someone describing themselves as David Beckham's assistant, who told him how people were expected to behave and dress at the soirée. He claimed he was specifically told not to come in his pink suit and that he felt he was virtually being told that he was not welcome. And so he did not go to the glittering affair. Instead, as the glittering bash unfolded at 'Beckingham Palace', Dave was at home watching TV and having a diet supper of cabbage soup. He was in the company, however, of three Russian girlfriends, so it was not an entirely wasted evening.

He consulted me, and I got on my white charger. He sued the Beckhams for defamation, alleging, amongst other things, that he had learned from a journalist that David and Victoria considered him to be something of an 'Arthur Daley' character.

Thursday, 19th July, 2007

QUEEN'S BENCH DIVISION

ROOM E119

Before MASTER LESLIE

Thursday, 19th July, 2007

At 10 o'clock

tech Europe Ltd v- Advance Enterprises Ltd

At half past 11

West & Another v- Beckham & Another

Dave lost the case, the judge ruling that the slight was not the Beckhams' responsibility because they had had no involvement in him buying the ticket, and Dave could not prove that David and Victoria Beckham had called him an Arthur Daley character themselves.

"*I've never been made to feel so inferior in my life*," West told the Daily Mail at the time. "*I paid a lot of money, and then, with 24 hours to go, I was told that I wasn't 'approved'.*"

Dave Loved Going To Court

You have heard above of a girlfriend, Jo, full name Joanna, who was Polish and aged twenty-three. Dave, at 57, fell in love. He spent £400,000 on Jo after meeting her in the smart London nightclub, Chinawhite in December 2001, and later proposed marriage with an expensive engagement ring in Saint-Tropez. He named his nightclub in her honour. His gifts included clothes and jewellery worth £120,000, including a £25,500 watch and a £18,000 car.

Unfortunately, Dave then fell out with Jo. He had given her £150,000 to buy a shop in her home country, Poland, for her future, only to find that she was spending it on high living. He took her to court to freeze her bank accounts. Despite going to court, he professed his love for her, and they made up. Good business for me!

King of the booze cruise spends £400,000 on his Polish beauty... then takes her to court

The former market trader from Romford, with a greying ponytail and a penchant for gaudy shirts, is besotted by his 23-year-old girlfriend and sees no reason to give her up – even though he is taking her to court to try to stop her spending his money.

West, founder of the money-spinning duty-free drinks warehouse EastEnders, in Calais, lavished £400,000 on Joanna Dudzik in the 15 months after they met in the smart London nightclub Chinawhite in December 2001.

He proposed with an expensive engagement ring in St Tropez and they travelled frequently, visiting exotic destinations including Hong Kong and Japan.

West, who boasts that he still buys his trousers from Marks & Spencer, had also bought her clothes and jewellery worth £120,000 – including a £25,500 watch – and an £18,000 car.

But his generosity with his beloved ran out when, according to his High Court writ, Dudzik pocketed £150,000 he gave her to buy a shop in her home country of Poland.

Now, with the High Court's help, he wants to stem the flow of cash, while insisting that they are still in love. West issued his writ at the end of February, preventing Dudzik disposing of any assets, including a property in Poland he bought for her. He also froze her bank account.

He has banned her from spending more than £350 a week on living expenses, and Dudzik could be jailed or fined for contempt of court if she breaks the order.

West told The Mail on Sunday that the legal action was 'much ado

EXPENSIVE TASTE: Dave West with girlfriend Joanna Dudzik and, top left, West the wine seller

Dave's legal troubles did not end there. In 2008, when he was 64, he and his wife Jo were accused of molesting a girl aged 14. The assault had supposedly taken place at his flat above his members' club in Jermyn Street, Mayfair. His wife was accused of holding the girl down. The case was dropped, but it did nothing to help Dave's descent into heavy drinking.

The Richest List

Dave was featured in the Sunday Times Rich List as being worth over £50 million, but his 'wealth' soon blossomed to make him a billionaire, and he is worth a hundred million on that same list. The actual definition of a billionaire is having a thousand million, but it seems these days just a paltry one hundred will suffice. Dave told me he was not happy with his place on the list and wanted to be thought of as much wealthier.

This proved to be incredibly easy, and all I did to help that process was to drop a few titbits to some journalists and the Sunday Times team, who swallowed it without checking. Tip to investors and bankers: be very wary of the Richest List.

The Murder

Following a drunken argument with his son (David West Jr), Dave died from a single knife wound to the heart on 12 December 2014. His son was arrested and subsequently charged with his murder. Fortified with several whiskeys in the club, during which David West Jr texted his girlfriend several times to say he was going to kill his father, he went next door to Dave's house and did just that. He then returned to the club, ordered a further whiskey and phoned the police, telling them what he had done.

Nearby resident actor Stephen Fry said that he heard "*horrifying screams*" coming from the house and later saw Dave's body being carried out.

David West Jr. was sentenced to 13-and-a-half years on 9 November 2015 for his father's murder. I did not advise him. Had I done so, I would have avoided his strategy of fighting the case on the basis that he felt forced to kill his domineering father. This is another example of someone being led by the nose and given dreadful legal advice when literally everything was at stake. He should have pleaded guilty, expressed remorse, obtained a private psychiatric report and come to me. I reckon I could have got him out in no more than eight years.

Nightclub heir jailed for killing bullying father

David Brown

From the age of 14 David West worked tirelessly for his father, living in the shadow of the garish pink suits worn by the booze-cruise entrepreneur turned nightclub impresario.

Then, just before last Christmas, he stabbed his father to death in a flat near one of their clubs.

As the once-loyal son was jailed yesterday, after he admitted killing "Lord" David West, 70, it emerged that his father had written him out of his will six years before his death. In the end, this final insult did not matter because the businessman, who once boasted of being worth £100 million, died penniless. West Jr, 45, admitted using a kitchen knife to stab his father, who was lying in a drunken stupor on the stairs of the flat above his Abracadabra restaurant in Mayfair, central London.

David West Jr said he endured years of verbal abuse from his father

He was jailed for 13 and a half years by a judge at the Old Bailey yesterday after admitting manslaughter by reason of loss of control. A jury had previously failed to reach a verdict on a murder charge. Nicholas Hilliard, QC, the Recorder of London, said: "It was clear that you suffered verbal abuse and verbal aggression … for many years."

told the court: "There was a toxic relationship between father and son. Although in latter years David West Sr was frail, he had an acerbic tongue that could reduce grown men to tears."

West, the eldest of three children, described his father as a "drunken bully" and said that their argument shortly before the stabbing was the first time he had stood up for himself.

"I have always loved my father but he has never been a father to me, he's always been my boss," he said.

His father liked to boast that when he left the Merchant Navy to work on a stall at Romford market in east London he was following a 400-year family tradition of market trading.

At the age of 25 he left Britain with his wife, Kathy, and moved to Belgium and later France to cash in on the boom in "booze cruises" by customers looking to buy cheap alcohol and cigarettes.

Mr West had claimed that in its heyday the family business had an annual turnover of £120 million before it collapsed in 2011. After his divorce, Mr West Sr had relationships with a string of young women and sought to enhance his social standing by buying the title of lordship of the manor of Hollesley, a village in Suffolk. In 2007 he hired Cherie Blair, QC, to mount an unsuccessful challenge against the ban on smoking in public places.

Oksana Stanzione, Mr West's PA and his son's former girlfriend, told the trial that she had witnessed the pair rowing on the day of the stabbing and Mr West confided in her: "This is my son … It's a shame. If I could I'd have hit him."

and told police: "I would like to admit to a murder. I've just killed my father."

The court was told that West Jr's mother and siblings had all been against a trial but the Crown had decided it was right to bring the evidence before a jury.

Days before the trial started, Mr West's will was published. Although he had left everything to charities, it transpired his debts outstripped his assets.

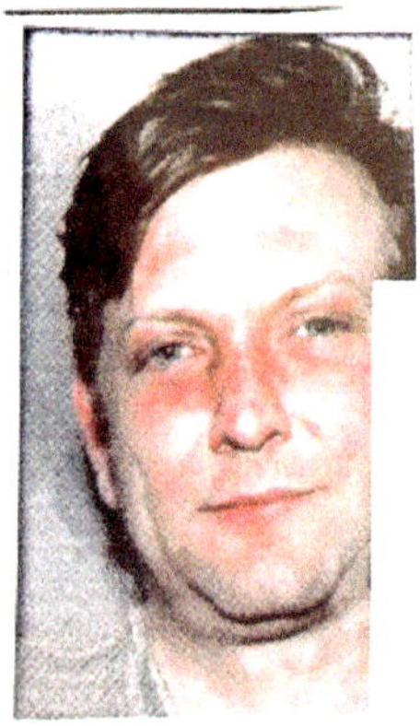

Dave was typical of the sort of client who turns to me, not a regulated solicitor, for advice. He did not want to be talked down to. He wanted somebody who had been through the mill, not sitting in some stuffy office, pompously giving 'arse-covering' legal advice.

Dave did not die in credit. He lived life to the full. You would have loved him.

RIP Dave. We miss you.

Rather than dwell on his tragic death, let me share with you a wonderful story about Dave, which you could not make up. While Cherie Booth and I continued to fight the smoking ban, Dave and all his customers smoked freely in his club. This attracted the attention of the Westminster City Council licensing enforcement team, who called him for an interview under caution one day at 3.00 pm.

My wife and legal partner, Maud, and I went to the club to pick him up, arriving at 2.00 pm, so we had time to prep him on the way to the interview, only to find that he was already very drunk. I laughed and said not a problem, we would postpone the interview. He would not hear of it, however, and off he went to the appointment with us, rather the worse for wear.

The audio tape was switched on, and the process started with the usual caution, which we have all seen a hundred times on TV. Before the interview had got very far, however, Dave turned to the rather feisty but attractive female Local Authority enforcement officer and said, "*After this interview is over, I intend to take you back to my club and fuck you.*"

I bent forward and said, "*For the benefit of the tape, Mr West is not referring to Mrs Maud Bergvelt*!"

The enforcement officer exploded with laughter. It is hard to be harsh with others when you are laughing.

From Hero To Zero

What is the difference between a lawyer and a vulture?

One is a rabid scavenger that feeds off unfortunates, and the other is a bird.

This book is not about me, or at least not much. I could not resist a bit. It is about the cases I have handled and the clients I have helped, but above all, it is about hope. There are so many ways that a good lawyer can help someone whose world seems to be falling apart. I only include these few lines about what happened to me to try to give hope to others when your life seems over and your world is shattered.

I was born in 1945, so I am 79 at the time of writing. I have one sister, Jacquie, a tower of strength. My father studied law and got a degree aged 42 - rare now and even rarer in 1952. At school, I played rugby for East Cheshire. There came a time, in about 1963, when padding was put around rugby goalposts. I was the last English schoolboy to break his nose on a rugby goalpost before padding was put up. Pretty pathetic claim to fame!

As a teenager, I was a Beatles fanatic. I followed them before they were famous and went to clubs and danced to their music in dance halls way before the big arenas. I sang along to '*She Loves You, Yeah, Yeah, Yeah'* with gusto and still do. Years later, I won a Times competition for the best description of the explosion that started every Beatles concert. Here it is:

A memory of Buxton Pavilion Gardens, 6 April 1963
You were no one unless you danced to the Beatles. Before they filled theatres with seats, Beatlemania filled dance halls. I saw them in Buxton. I handed in all my savings of £5 in exchange for an autograph from Paul McCartney - a girl lost an eye in the scrum, a terrible tragedy, but I shall never forget when those curtains opened. The atmosphere was utterly electric, the sound different. Every boy there wanted to be and sing like a Beatle. Every girl wanted to be a Beatles girl.

It sounds trite, but those who did not experience dancing with the Beatles live can never possibly understand why everyone else - Michael Jackson, the Spice Girls, Madonna, Oasis - are also-rans.
Rodney Hylton-Potts

Reading it, even today, makes the hairs on the back of my neck stick up. They really were amazing.

In 1963, I left school, aged 18, to start a five-year course, or 'articles', to train as a solicitor (three years earlier than most students). I had no desire to go to university. I wanted to get started. In 1966, I went to court for the first time as a trainee. Our client had drunk 10 pints and admitted following the white line on the road in his car to get home, but the jury acquitted him. '*There but for the grace of God,'* they must have thought.

The law introducing the breathalyser came into force in 1967. Before that, I was utterly irresponsible (as were all my friends). I have driven a sports car after ten pints. I have driven home after golf and after a boozy lunch and several Kummels.

I thank God every day that I did not kill anybody, especially a child - more by luck than judgment. Two of my friends actually did kill people when behind the wheel, one a child.

When an adult drives a child or family in a car, it is a sacred trust to look after them and to keep them safe. That is a fundamental obligation of being a parent. Looking back, I am thoroughly ashamed of how I did the exact opposite behind the wheel.

When the breathalyser came in, I behaved myself and never drank and drove again. It is an excellent law that definitely has saved lives. My shame, however, will never leave me.

Qualification And My First Big Case

On 24 April 1970, aged just 24, I qualified as a solicitor and quickly burst onto the legal scene. Within a few weeks of qualifying, I was featured on the front page of The Times, representing five members of The Amalgamated Union of Engineers who took legal action against their union. The wonderful Times headline read, '*Last night Mr Hylton-Potts was visited by five men'.* I was teased mercilessly.

The union were trying to impose one-day strikes (political strikes). That means a strike whose object is not an employment advantage but a political advantage. The Unions were trying to bring down the government and were quite open about it.

Some hard-left activists in the Trade Union movement wanted to have a greater and more direct say and influence on the way the country was governed. This was generally hedged about with rhetoric about better working conditions, higher pay, more holidays, etc., but this was only a smokescreen.

It was also a time when one factory might have as many as 10 trade unions representing the workforce, and the more active or 'militant' representatives wished to make a mark for themselves. This caused a great deal of chaos and can be contrasted with, for example,

Germany, where there tends to be one union representing all the workers at one workplace.

Anyway, the UK is set up in such a way that we vote for MPs, and the party that can command a majority in Parliament forms the government to govern the country. We do not want to be governed by Trade Unions who have not been elected to Parliament. Many Labour MPs were, and some still are, sponsored by Trade Unions. The Unions own the Labour party.

The five clients were recommended to me by a high-profile MP, Airey Neave, who was later blown up by a bomb in the House of Commons slip road leading out of the underground car park. He was MP for Abingdon near Oxford, near where I worked after I qualified and a personal friend and favourite of the Prime Minister, Margaret Thatcher. The press was obsessed with trying to find out whether the Tory party were paying the legal fees of the five men, who could not possibly have afforded me, and more importantly, Alec Campbell, a top QC I was told to brief. I learnt early on about private detectives rummaging through dustbins.

It was all great fun, and in one of the court hearings before the famous Lord Denning, he was reading a handwritten Affidavit of mine, observing that it was sticky and appeared to have marmalade on it. Indeed, it did, as I had written it out overnight and had a hasty breakfast of marmalade on toast before setting off to the Court of Appeal in the Strand in London.

Young lawyers and executives boast about '*pulling an all-nighter*', but it usually is just posturing because they were not properly prepared. Anyhow, if you ever do one, have a cooked breakfast or at least avoid marmalade on toast!

Heady Days

In 1974, I married Gilly, and we have three grown-up children. The eldest, Silvie, is my pride and joy; she is in a caring profession, which she loves. We lived in St George's Hill, Weybridge, Surrey, the most exclusive housing estate in Europe. The work flowed in. I even represented people whose names ended with a vowel.

After a divorce, I acquired a new wife, Suzanne, two more children, a house in Knightsbridge near Harrods (which locals called 'the corner shop'), a 100-acre stud farm in Berkshire, a black Rolls Royce with the personal number plate RHP 11, a mistress, a liking for glamourous clubs (like Annabel's) and West End restaurants. Holidays were in the South of France, at upmarket ski resorts like Zermatt or Antigua in the Caribbean.

I was a member of the Society of Conservative Lawyers, appeared on TV and mixed easily with politicians and merchant bankers.

My clients included a Saudi Arabian Sheik and the brother of the arms dealer 'Mr Fixit' Adnan Khashoggi, John Lennon's psychiatrist and Asil Nadar's stockbroker (see below, the Polly Peck, a scandal which rocked Mrs Thatcher's government).

Sheik sues over coaches

By RICHARD MILNER

A SAUDI Arabian sheik plans to sue the National Bus Company, threatening to stop the Government's £100 million-plus privatisation programme.

Sheik Omar Khashoggi, related to arms dealer 'Mr Fix-It' Adnan Khashoggi, ordered 200 second-hand coaches from the NBC last year to take pilgrims to the holy city of Mecca. He claims he specified the buses should be air-conditioned — and they weren't. 'Not only was there no air-conditioning, his solicitor said: 'even the windows wouldn't open.'

Sheik Khashoggi is suing the National Bus Company for £13 million — NBC is disputing the claim.

By coincidence, the subsidiary that handled this Saudi deal — NBC Consultancy Services — has already been wound down and its chief executive, Tom Glass, is off sick.

So far, the NBC has sold off 13 of its 71 area companies for an undisclosed sum. And Omar Khashoggi is in no mood to end up suing an empty shell with no money.

'If the writ does not get the National Bus Company to the negotiating table', said solicitor Rodney Hylton-Potts, 'we will apply for an injunction to freeze its assets.'

'That could stop NBC privatisation for up to two years, Conservative Government or no Conservative Government,' he added. 'And it won't improve British relations with Saudi Arabia.'

<u>Girls</u>

When I was 42, between marriages, I took out my secretary, Lavinia, aged 21. Oldest story in the book. I was a bit like a legal Rupert Cambell-Black, or at least so I thought.

Her father was a senior client of the firm and captain of a very exclusive golf club. His name was Hugo. Debonair, with silver hair, was the most delightful man you could meet, the original Silver Fox.

Shortly after taking Lavinia away for a weekend, he invited me to play golf at his club, and I readily accepted. It is a very famous golf club, and his companionship was brilliant. All went well until the fourth hole when he suddenly stopped me before I was about to play a shot. He said in his beautiful, clipped voice, "*I gather you have been taking my daughter, Lavinia, out to London clubs, restaurants and discotheques.*" He said "*discotheques*" with an "o", disc**o**theques.

Until that moment, I had called him Hugo, but 'Sir' sprang to my lips. He went on, "*I have just one thing to say to you, young man.*" Pause. I could feel my hands shaking on the club. "*It's bloody expensive, isn't it?*"

Inevitably, I hit an appalling golf shot, never recovered and lost the match.

Slow Lawyers

Lawyers are notoriously slow. Not me, and word soon got out. Of course, care must be taken, but a good rule is never to allow the same piece of paper to cross your desk twice. I have never come across anybody who works as quickly as I do. I am rather proud of the following letter I received in 1988 from a Senior Judge.

from: The Hon. Mr. Justice Michael Davies

ROYAL COURTS OF JUSTICE
STRAND, LONDON, WC2A 2LL

30 March 1988.

Dear Sirs,

As Judge in Charge of the Lists, I have since the beginning of this year been reviewing many cases as they are set down in the Queen's Bench Division non-Jury List.

These include medical negligence cases and I have been disturbed to find that in a random sample the average time from cause of action to setting down has been just over 7 years and as most of these cases require a fixed date an average of something like 8½ years is elapsing between the case of action and trial. This seems to me to be very unjust to Plaintiffs and also to doctors and others who are accused of negligence. Also, I suspect that the lay persons involved erroneously often think that a large part of the delay is due to the courts.

I understand that medical negligence cases are often difficult to prepare but I do not believe that delays need to be as long as they often are.

In these circumstances, I was so impressed to read the dates in the above mentioned case that I thought it only fair to send this congratulatory note.

They appear to be:

Cause of action	June 1986
Writ	3 November 1987
Order for Directions	29 February 1988
Set Down	24 March 1988

I see no reason why most of these cases should take more than 17 months before the writ is issued no more than 21 months from cause of action to setting down. Indeed this could be improved upon but, if I may say so, you have done so much better than the vast majority of these cases.

No doubt the Defendants Solicitors have also been co-operative and I am sending a copy of this letter to them.

Furthermore, I am letting the Clerk of the Lists have a copy. If there is an application for a fixture, please remind him of it: you deserve Rolls Royce treatment.

Yours truly,

Judge in Charge of the Lists.

Messrs. Hylton-Potts,
7, Cheval Place, London, S.W.7.
Copies to:
Messrs. Bircham & Co.,
1 Dean Farrer Street, London. SW1H 0DY
Clerk of the Lists.

Filling The Tory Coffers

Jason Davis was the stockbroker to Asil Nadir, who ran a glamorous company called 'Polly Peck' in the eighties. He was one of Margaret Thatcher's favourite industrialists and a big donor to the Tory Party.

At its height, Polly Peck had net assets of £845 million and over 17,000 employees. But then Asil put his hand in the till and began transferring money to his Cyprus companies, which led to the collapse of Polly Peck. In 1990, the Serious Fraud Office raided the company's offices during working hours. They found the lady financial director in bed with the company's bank manager! A novel way to apply for a loan. Also, some very suspicious share transactions emerged. Enter his stockbroker.

Jason was an Essex boy, handsome, dressed to impress with gold cuff links in French cuffs on his shirts. He chain-smoked, had expensive tastes and had a pretty Swiss wife.

In 1991, Jason was living in Tenerife and was the subject of an enquiry by the Serious Fraud Office, alleging that he had conspired with Asil Nadir to rig stock markets and indulge in insider trading. It was a big case, with complex facts and thousands of documents, and the Serious Fraud Office put huge resources into getting him.

He was struggling to pay my legal fees, so I arranged to raise the money from the News of the World for his story. I flew to Tenerife to arrange an interview with him with a hilarious journalist from the News of the World. The interview went something like this:

Journo: *You worked for Asil Nadir?*

Jason: *Yes.*

Journo: *Did he like parties?*

Jason: *Not really, although at Christmas, he would have a family get-together and a glass of champagne.*

Journo: *So that was a party?*

Jason: I suppose so.

Journo: *How many years did you work for him?*

Jason: *Four.*

Journo: *So there were several parties?*

Jason: *Yes*

Journo: *These parties you are talking about. Was alcohol served?*

Jason: *Not a lot. Asil worked very hard, although there would be a glass of champagne with the family.*

Journo: *So alcohol was served.*

Jason: *Yes.*

Journo: *Were any of the parties a bit wild?*

Jason: *They went on quite late.*

Journo: *These wild parties you are talking about. Were there any Tory politicians at them?*

Jason: *Yes, a couple of MPs were there with their wives, having a Christmas drink.*

Journo: That wraps it up. Thanks.

Based on that interview, the headline was:

Tory Donors Fill Coffers at Champagne-Fuelled Asil Nadir Parties!

The Truth About Drugs

During this period, the general public heard far more about drug taking than in previous years.

Because there is a lot of ignorance, let me tell you about drugs. Parents who pontificate and say to their children that all drugs are evil are talking rubbish. I would say that children should actually try drugs (other than heroin, Tusi or crack) to be educated. They will not get hooked. There is no need to worry.

Heroin

Heroin is incredibly dangerous, damaging and highly illegal. Never go near it. If you find your child taking it, report him or her to the police, as it will probably save their lives.

Cocaine

Cocaine gives a high. It is exhilarating and will make you feel confident and lose your inhibitions. Mixed with alcohol, the feeling is supposed to be fantastic but addictive. It is to be handled with the greatest care, however, because it can lead to breakups of friendships and marriages, poor decisions and poor health, including heart attacks. At the simplest level, the taker will not be able to sleep and will be in no fit state to work effectively the next day. The price has remained steady at about £50 a gram for many years. With inflation, that means the price has dropped. The war on drugs is lost, so we should stop fighting it.

I had a friend called Wilfred, who was 72. He watched my girlfriend sniffing lines of cocaine and asked what it cost. She said about £5 a line. He said that was ridiculous and a glass of good wine was a better bet.

Intrigued, however, he decided to try it. He sniffed two big lines and waited. He then began to talk rapidly: *"Would you like to hear about my ex-wife? Total bitch."* And off he went. After about five minutes, he stopped and said, *"That is a complete waste of money. I feel completely normal. On the other hand, I have never felt normal before!"*

Crack Cocaine

This is mainly taken on sink estates and is incredibly addictive. It should never be tried, but I am told the only way to try it, if you must, is to take a standard cigarette, empty out about one-third and then sprinkle cocaine inside. Then, lick the side of the cigarette paper to make it burn slowly and light it. I am told the effect is extraordinary. It hits the brain in about five seconds (compared with perhaps 30 seconds for sniffed cocaine) and gives an immediate high. So far, so good. The problem is that about 20 minutes later when the effect is wearing off and you 'come down,' there is a second buzz, which is even better. That is extremely addictive, which is why it should never be tried at all or only once. People addicted in that way will do anything. They would leave work, an important social gathering, a dying relative, a funeral, anything to get more.

Pink Cocaine

Pink cocaine, known as 'Tusi', should also be avoided, as much as heroin or crack cocaine. It is a dangerous mix of drugs, a cocktail with compounds similar to fentanyl, a cheaper synthetic opioid many times stronger than heroin. It is literally a killer as Liam Payne, a pop star from the group One Direction, discovered in 2024.

Marijuana And Hash

Marijuana (grass) and hash are smoked all over the world regularly and, frankly, are no more addictive or bad for you than a glass of wine. Absolute rubbish is talked about as grass or hash, and it should be legalised, regulated and taxed, as in some places in the world. To criminalise somebody who has a joint while his brother has a glass of wine, making one a criminal and one a connoisseur, is pure rubbish and should be embarrassing to governments.

Ecstasy

It is said that a million ecstasy pills are taken a week in Britain. Most of them are cheap, safe and give a buzz when dancing in a club, although a lot of water must be drunk. Then there are the more expensive ones such as 'Mitsubishis', which cause a huge high. It causes you to look at the other person with a huge wage of love but then say something that someone with Tourette Syndrome might say. You might say, for example, *"I love you so much. I have not felt able to say it before. I long to make you my wife and love you forever, if only your nose wasn't so big."*

Smash And Grab

There are far more guns in police cars in London and major cities than the public realises. They are tightly controlled, and to be able to withdraw a firearm from a glovebox where it is held, special permission has to be given. In the late 90s, I was involved in a case where a jeweller was robbed in Bond Street. An 'all-cars alert' went out and was picked up by a nearby police car. The driver was told the facts, and he said they could get to the shop within two minutes, but he would need permission (under Rule 22) to withdraw the firearm from the glove box. This was given.

The case went to court. The police officer driver gave evidence.

"I was called to the shop having withdrawn my revolver from the glovebox under the authority of Rule 22. A robbery was in progress. I could see the accused (a black man) in the shop holding up the staff, terrorising the staff. I shouted out, 'Armed Police. Lay down your weapons. I was ignored.

I shouted louder, 'Armed Police lay down your weapons'.

I was ignored, so I shot him."

A later witness was the shop assistant, who told a slightly different story.

"I was working in Bond Street when the Defendant burst in and terrorised me and the staff. We were very frightened. He demanded we open the safe and empty the jewels and watches into a bag that he had. Not two minutes later, a police officer burst in, looked at him and said, 'Good night, Sooty,' and shot him."

Clever People

I had a client who bought some land on the sea in Norfolk. He applied for planning permission to build a modest bungalow.

The owner of a large house inland objected on the grounds that even a bungalow would spoil his view of the sea, which was actually a fair point.

Most people would have given up, but not this client. He literally took a long-term view. He planted a row of Italian Cypress, fast-growing trees, well inside his boundary and waited. Within four years, they had grown to such a height that the neighbour had no view of the sea at all.

He put in an application for planning, and the neighbour's objection was, this time, brushed aside.

Why did he not grow the trees right up against the boundary? Experience shows that poison is used a lot when trees come into play. Particularly, a tree with a Tree Preservation Order on it can certainly find itself being killed by poison, which is almost undetectable, whereas a machine or axe in the middle of the night could lead to an arrest. Never underestimate how clever, even devious, successful people can be.

Success and Disaster

I suppose, looking back, I felt invincible, as many people would in my situation. I am not suggesting that I was powerful or in the league of people like Lord Jeffrey Archer or Jonathan Aitkin, but many Alpha Male types feel invincible and use their money to buy their way out of trouble again and again. I suppose I was part of the way down that road. I certainly was arrogant and took my eye off the ball. Disaster lay ahead.

"Nothing personal, Mr Knight, but I was hoping to speak to one of the others."

The Cemetery Deal

In 1986, by which time I had my own solicitors firm in Knightsbridge near Harrods, London, I met John Whybrow, a property developer and wheeler-dealer, who was my downfall. Westminster Council were losing money on three cemeteries in Highgate at the rate of some £400,000 p.a. They were a pointless financial burden, but the land included lodges, houses and grazing land for possible development for housing, which had not been properly factored in. Through various overseas companies, John

Whybrow bought the cemeteries for 5p each, and the joke was "*Time was you could go up West, buy a pint and three cemeteries and still get change from a fiver*".

Westminster Council foolishly sold against a promise to keep the graves in good condition, which was immediately ignored. I remember the Billy Fury fan club was angry as the late pop star's grave was untended.

It's WAR! Cemetery relatives protest outside
Marylebone Council House.

Whybrow bought and sold the cemeteries, clearing £600,000 profit without putting up a penny.

Eventually, Westminster Counsel re-acquired the land by paying £4.25m. The deal was legal, but I was so well paid by Whybrow that I took my eye off the ball. He became my best client, and I became careless and dropped my guard.

I discovered much later that Whybrow, apart from being a fiendishly clever negotiator, was also basically a crook and had a criminal conviction for cheque fraud, which he had hidden from me. He did not even own his house, and I assumed too much. He lived in a beautiful house in St John's Wood, which, freehold, would have been worth about £750,000 in those days, about 1986. I had no idea that he was merely a Rent Act sitting tenant, and his tenancy had no value. I should have checked. No excuse. Just stupid. I was careless and trusting. I was not drafting wills in Berkshire. I was a big London player, riding for a fall.

Whybrow wanted a Panamanian company, probably to do the deal tax-free. I had several 'on the shelf' (they were literally in a cabinet in my office). I picked one out at random, called Chelwood Holdings Ltd. It could just as easily have been Alpha Investments or Zebra Developments. By one of those extraordinary coincidences, Dame Shirley Porter (who was chairwoman of Westminster Council and wife of a Tesco heir) lived in a house called Chelwood House and had an offshore company called Chelwood Nominees. The press got hold of it and thought she had to be in on the deal. She ended up on the run and in exile in Israel. Real life in action.

The Scottish Hotel Fraud

Later in the 1990s, I helped Whybrow set up a scheme of companies to buy three Scottish hotels. Whybrow and I were charged with defrauding the banks, who lent money on the deal. I rejected any suggestion of a plea deal. The jury had a choice to decide whether I had just been careless or crooked.

They decided I had been crooked, and I was sentenced in 1996 to five years in jail, of which I served two and a half.

Whybrow committed the classic mortgage fraud of acquiring properties by putting a company in the middle. It looked as though he was putting up deposits, but he was not. The commercial reality was, however, that the banks could not care less. It was a 'tick box' situation, and the banks were not interested. All they wanted to hear about was a good title and valuation. The matter came home to roost when the hotel group collapsed about three years later; the 'tick box' was all forgotten, and there was a rush to find an interpretation of dishonesty.

The bank managers ran for cover. One example: during the Scottish hotels deal, I invited the bankers for drinks in the famous Loose Box wine bar, Knightsbridge, which was underneath my office. This was just a way of doing business (today, we would call it networking), but later, it was made to look like I was procuring a girl for the bankers. One of my friends who dropped in was a jolly blonde called Gill, who was also my hairdresser. The bankers thought she was great fun and happily went off somewhere in a taxi with her. Their delight got conveniently forgotten at the trial.

The jury heard of my Rolls Royce, champagne and foreign travel and did not like what they heard, nor did they understand the case, as often happens in fraud cases. They concluded that there must be something to it (no smoke without fire), and what were we doing in court on a fraud charge anyway if we were innocent?

Juries

There is a perception that a jury is a bunch of unemployed layabouts who come in from the rain for £80 a day and just skive and nod off. This is simply not true. Juries take their responsibilities extremely seriously. They have a nose for dishonesty and bring their common sense and experience of the world to a trial.

It is a fantastic system. The problem today is that the practice of juries asking questions has died out. Up to about the 1960s, if a member of a jury did not understand something or felt a question had been missed by the barristers, they would ask a question themselves. It is a terrible pity that this has died out. It often showed the shortcomings of the barristers in that they had missed a pertinent question to ask.

Whybrow's defence was that I was the 'Mr Big'. He said it was my money. He claimed that I had bought the hotels. He said I owned his house in Spain and that he was just a consultant working for me. I controlled his funds through offshore Trust arrangements on his behalf, but he said the funds were mine. The judge and jury did not believe a word of it, and none of what he claimed was true.

On the penultimate day of the trial, Whybrow wore a wire in the Court café before a conversation with me in an effort to show that I was indeed this 'Mr Big'. He tried to trap me into asking him to take the blame in exchange for looking after his family when he was in prison. His barrister tried to get the judge to listen to the recording, but the judge was not interested. He did himself no favours. It was very clear who the real Mr Big was.

In my case, the jury had two options. They could either conclude that I was stupid and negligent or dishonest. They decided I was too clever to be that stupid, so I must be dishonest. I should never have allowed myself to get in that position.

When we were both sent to the same prison, Whybrow's evil did not stop there. He caused me to be thrown out of an open prison (by 'grassing' me up for running a business) after he discovered I was helping an old client with a will. I ended up back in Brixton.

I would not recommend prison to anybody, but I learned a huge amount, and it made me the fighter I am today, determined that nothing like that will ever befall my clients.

Vote For Rodders

In 2004, Maud, my wife and partner in our legal practice, spotted an advertisement in one of the Sunday papers inviting applicants to enter a political reality show on ITV called 'Vote For Me'. Applicants had to send in a manifesto. Mine included a complete ban on immigration and the castration of paedophiles.

Here it is:

1. Immigration
Great Britain is full when it comes to asylum seekers and immigration. We are closed for business. Send illegal aliens home, with immediate deportation for overstayers.

2. Population
Policies aimed to reduce the population by one-third within 25 years.

3. Child Allowances
Whilst providing a safety net for very poor families, no family or tax allowances for children.

4. Europe

Withdraw totally from political and economic ties. Never join the Euro. Repeal European Community Act (1972) (I was a very early Brexiteer).

5. Crime

Massive building programme - only prison works. Legalise, regulate and tax all drugs other than heroin and crack cocaine. Enforced castration for child molesters.

6. Daylight hours

Permanent British summertime with double British summertime in summer.

7. Divorce/Children

Presumption of 50/50 split of time children spend with separated parents. (This has since become law)*. Binding pre-nuptial agreements.*

8. Human Rights

Repeal the Human Rights Act and leave ECHR.

After winning various preliminary rounds (in heats contested over five one-hour programmes at 11 pm on ITV on consecutive nights),

I won the final with a massive 85% of the vote. The judges tried to vote me off each night for a week, and Martin Bell, the political reporter, called me a "*Silver-tongued extremist*" while clearly thinking a great deal worse than that.

There was lots of fun behind the scenes. The first thing was the betting. The crew could see straight away that I was almost certain to win because I was outrageous, and the ratings were soaring. I could tell what the viewers wanted and gave it to them. The crew later told me they had all put money on me, and I put money on myself, at 25 to 1. My family and friends, and even a decorator who was in the middle of decorating my kitchen, were all dispatched to bookie shops to put bets on me before they closed the books.

I worked out what the producers wanted. For example, each contestant was given surprise questions to see if they were a 'man/woman of the people'. One question was, "*How much is a pint of milk?*" Other contestants gave replies like *"£1"*, but I replied, *"I do not know myself, but my butler will know."* I also said that the best way to help the poor was to not be one of them.

I followed the KISS mantra when answering questions. Keep it simple, stupid.

The contestants went on a coach canvassing in the poorest area of Liverpool. We had to knock on doors, explaining we were in a reality show, and ask for their vote. One contestant was called Dominic Carman, son of the famous QC George Carman. My wife Maud overheard him whilst we were being checked into the team hotel, loudly boasting that he would win the show without a doubt.

Unfortunately for him, he turned out to be a grey and boring politician and was the first contestant to be sent home on day one. He was furious that I had won and tried to get his revenge by telling the press details of a conversation in which he claimed I had said: "*There was a time when you could drive out to Henley-on-Thames, have a pub lunch and drive back any time without traffic and not a n..... on the streets*." This caused something of a media frenzy, but it was soon forgotten because it was obviously not true. It was all rather a shame because I did and do very much admire his fantastic late father. The following was typical.

ROW ERUPTS AS TV's NEW POLITICAL IDOL ACCUSED OF BEING RACIST

An innovative attempt to revitalise the public's interest in politics by subjecting would-be MPs to a Pop Idol-style reality TV show descended into ugly scenes last night after the winner was accused of holding views to the right of the British National Party. Rodney Hylton-Potts, who has served two years in Brixton prison for fraud, should have been spending this weekend celebrating his Friday night victory in the ITV Vote For Me competition.

Instead, he is being forced to deny allegations that he told a fellow competitor that in the 1960s, "you could drive to Henley without seeing a n......r on the streets." Hylton-Potts, who won the completion on the strength of what he calls his 'cabbie's manifesto' - the mandatory castration of paedophiles, the legalisation of all drugs, the repeal of the human rights act, a massive prison-building scheme and an immigrant deportation programme that would reduce Britain's population by 20 million, vehemently denies the allegation.

Last night, the 59-year-old solicitor accused one of the contestants he defeated, Dominic Carman, son of the famous libel lawyer George Carman, of staging a campaign against him.
"Dominic Carman is going around Fleet Street making very, very serious allegations against me," said Hylton-Potts, who is now planning to stand as an independent MP in the next election.

The punitive politician, a favourite of former Sun editor Kevin MacKenzie, who was one of the show's three judges - alongside television host Lorraine Kelly and ex-ITN political editor John Sergeant - said: "After I won, I went out to celebrate at a restaurant with friends, including one of my best friends, who is a Muslim from Kenya."

A Showdown With The Producers

I had supporters who were often friends of my family and students who had travelled quite a long way to support me at the evening 11.00 pm show in London. Before the show, my wife Maud treated them to drinks in a pub over the road, and they got very enthusiastic as the evening wore on, particularly so during the live broadcasts every night. On the penultimate show, I was told by the producers that they were making too much noise and could not come in on the final night. I protested, but they said it was no use and they would not be allowed in. I said to myself, "*We will see about that.*"

We had a rehearsal on the last night, whereby some of the TV crew played the part of the three judges. The judges were Kelvin McKenzie (former editor of 'The Sun'), John Sargeant (political commentator) and Lorraine Kelly (TV presenter). In this mock rehearsal, I told the mock judges that on live TV that night, I planned to challenge the judges on whether they had taken drugs in the last 28 days and demand that snips of their hair be taken in the studio and analysed. The result would be broadcast on Lorraine's live show the following week.

Word of my bizarre plan got back to the real judges, and they backed off big time. I was told that my supporters could all attend after all. This told me a lot.

My clampdown on immigration was wildly popular with the public. Remember, this was 2005, and I was a lonely voice in the wilderness. I could count on the fingers of the right hand of a Finsbury Park Muslim cleric the number of people who wanted increased immigration.

I went for the "cabby" vote, pointing out that if you want to know what the public thinks, ask a cabby. I thought that then, and I think it now.

The Castration Of Paedophiles

In one dramatic moment, Kelvin McKenzie asked me how I planned to castrate the paedophiles. I said, "*With two bricks". "And who would do it?*' I said, "*She is sitting right behind you*". At that moment, the camera panned in on my wife, Maud, in the audience behind Kelvin. She motioned with her hands as if cracking two bricks together. I was told later that the voting machines almost burnt out!

After winning, I was asked on live TV if I could think of anybody who had gone straight from prison to become a politician. I said "*Nelson Mandela*" but was told they were more thinking of 'Adolf Hitler'.

After winning Vote for Me, the Daily Mail wrote an article about me titled: ***Is this the reborn Dutch politician Pym Fortuyn and his moll?***

The Mirror Picked Up On My Cabbie Vote Theme

Cabbies, both in London and elsewhere, are not alone in holding passionate views about how to put the world to rights. But unlike the rest of us, the ranting taxi driver is always blessed with a ready audience: the paying passenger.

Cabbies' friend? Rodney Hylton-Potts

This potent combination of hard-edged rightist politics and a willingness to spout them at every opportunity seems to have inspired Rodney Hylton-Potts, winner of ITV's 'Vote for Me'.

The show, which ran last week, was a Pop Idol-style contest in which viewers voted for budding MPs. Mr Hylton-Potts, a convicted fraudster and former solicitor, won on a manifesto that included halting immigration, the mandatory castration of paedophiles, the repeal of the Human Rights Act, the legalisation of all drugs and a massive prison-building scheme.

"*I won because of what I call the cabbie vote*," Mr Hylton-Potts said later, describing how his policies had been influenced by the cab drivers who drove him to and from the studios during the making of the show.

"*I think cabbies are a very good guide. When I told them my views, every single one of them said, 'Good on you, mate'.*"

Martin Bell Hits Back

Is this silver-tongued extremist really what the voters want?

By MARTIN BELL, Mail on Sunday

When the idea was first put to me, I liked the sound of it. Vote For Me - a sort of cross between Pop Idol and Question Time - would be a new kind of political television.

It would engage voters, especially the young and those untouched by the dreary routines of party politics. It would be the nearest thing to a party political broadcast ever made by the Independents. That certainly got my vote.

People with political ambitions but no party allegiances were asked to put themselves forward as Independents, with a view to standing at the next election in a constituency of their choice.

Their ideas, manifestos and abilities would all be tested on the programme.

A thousand hopefuls applied, to be reduced by a panel of judges to the seven who appeared on television last week. At that point, the judges' powers ran out. The winners would be picked by the viewers, as happens on the wilder shores of reality television.

The opening programme featured all kinds of eccentrics, including a Druid, a former porn star and a candidate who sang his manifesto to an excruciating guitar accompaniment.

In a radio debate the next morning, Sir Bernard Ingham, Lady Thatcher's former Press secretary, condemned it as a parade of weirdos and nutters.

To which I replied that there are a fair number of those in the House of Commons already, many occupying some of the safest seats.

The first of the seven candidates was voted out, and the next day, I had a walk-on part as the remaining six took a master class on how to survive in the house as an Independent. Their principal tutor was Richard Taylor, MP for Kidderminster, who was elected on a democratic landslide in 2001 as the voters protested against the near-closure of their hospital.

Dr Taylor was a single-issue candidate, but in the house, he is a multi-issue MP. He speaks and votes across the whole political waterfront. He is highly effective and well respected.

Watching the edited version that night, I was aware that the ITV project was falling apart. It wasn't the fault of the candidates.

Most were serious and electable. It was the fault of the judges. The chairman, political journalist John Sergeant, was looking for someone who could play the Westminster game. To the right of him, in every sense, was Kelvin MacKenzie, former editor of The Sun. He wanted a populist, an anti-politician with the ferocity of a tabloid leader-writer. A candidate whose issue was honest politics didn't make the shortlist.

So it was that the final seven - then six, then five, then four, then three, then two - included Rodney Hylton-Potts, a 58-year-old former solicitor from London. He stood out from the rest as a candidate of conviction. It was a conviction for mortgage fraud, for which he served two-and-a-half years of a five-year sentence.

He was open about his criminal record. He explained disarmingly that, unlike the Conservatives' A-Team of Archer and Aitken, at least he'd done his time at Her Majesty's pleasure before getting into Parliament.

What also set him apart was his manifesto. Mr Hylton-Potts denies being a racist or fascist. But on immigration, he seems to stand to the right of the BNP. He is an extreme Little Englander. He wishes to send all asylum seekers and their children home. "We're full," he says. "We're closed for business."

He seeks to cut our island's population by a third over 25 years. He proposes a massive prison-building programme and castration for child offenders.

The former fraudster went down well with the studio audience - he is a confident performer and 'character' who would fit rather well into the House of Commons. There are lots of MPs like him. He reminds me of a more extreme and aggressive Neil Hamilton.

By the end of Wednesday's programme, the judges were worrying. By Thursday, they were panicking. On successive nights, even Kelvin MacKenzie urged the viewers to reject Mr Hylton-Potts. The viewers paid no attention. On Friday night, he was chosen as the people's champion - a victory for silver-tongued extremism. He has yet to choose his constituency for the General Election. But an established politician out there somewhere could be in for a bit of a shock.

Unlike most reality TV shows, I doubt if Vote For Me will have a sequel or celebrity version. It caused too much heartache in the network. It had too many lawyers crawling all over it, looking for breaches of the Representation of the People Act.

But it raised an interesting democratic question: if Mr Hylton-Potts's opinions are widely held among voters as well as viewers, shouldn't they be fully represented in the House of Commons - within the law, of course?

I trust that Dr Taylor wins his deserved re-election in Kidderminster. If he doesn't, and Rodney Hylton-Potts becomes the lone Independent standard-bearer in the house, I may finally have to break a long habit and seek refuge in a political party.

And 'Racist' Was Trotted Out In The Press

Row erupts as TV's new political idol is accused of being racist.

Jamie Doward, *Social Affairs Editor*

Sunday 16 January 2005

An innovative attempt to revitalise the public's interest in politics by subjecting would-be MPs to a Pop Idol-style reality TV show descended into ugly scenes last night after the winner was accused of holding views to the right of the British National Party.

Rodney Hylton-Potts, who has served two years in Brixton prison for fraud, should have been spending this weekend celebrating his Friday night victory in ITV's Vote For Me competition.

But instead, he is being forced to deny allegations that he told a fellow competitor that in the 1960s, 'you could drive to Henley without seeing a nigger on the streets'.

Hylton-Potts, who won the competition on the strength of what he calls his 'cabbie's manifesto' - the mandatory castration of paedophiles, the legalisation of all drugs, the repeal of the human rights act, a massive prison-building scheme and an immigrant deportation programme that would reduce Britain's population by 20 million - vehemently denies the allegation.

Last night, the 59-year-old solicitor accused one of the six finalists whom he defeated, Dominic Carman, son of the famous libel lawyer George Carman, of staging a campaign against him.

'Dominic Carman is going around Fleet Street making very, very serious allegations against me,' said Hylton-Potts, who is now planning to stand as an independent MP at the next election.

The putative politician, a favourite of former Sun editor Kelvin MacKenzie, who was one of the show's three judges - alongside television host Lorraine Kelly and ex-ITN political editor John Sergeant - denied being racist.

'After I won, I went out to celebrate at a restaurant with one of my greatest mates who is from Kenya and a Muslim,' he said.

But he admitted that his anti-immigration stance was the chief reason for his success.

'I won because of what I call the "cabbie vote", he said. 'I think cabbies are a very good guide. As I was being ferried back and forth to the studio, I would say to the cabby: 'What do you think of immigration?'

'When I told them my views, every single one of them said: "Good on you, mate."'

Last night, Carman accused Hylton-Potts of winning by 'galvanising a racist, anti-immigrant vote' and questioned whether the judges should have allowed him to enter the final.

'Putting forward a comedy fascist as a serious candidate was always going to be playing with fire. It gives a voice to extremism in the name of entertainment,' Carman said.

An ITV spokesman defended the programme.

'It achieved what it set out to achieve, which was to raise the level of debate about politics and engage people in the process.

'It was watched by a million people every night, and tens of thousands of people voted in the final.'

Standing As An MP

After winning the reality show, I had my 15 minutes of fame. 'Newsnight' with Jeremy Paxman, Sky News, LBC and BBC radio followed. The question was always, '*Are you a racist?*' See https://www.youtube.com/watch?v=Fm216gsYHso

Few feel comfortable saying it, but the truth is that the average Brit just wants to live in a predominantly British country with familiar people and things around him or her. We are a tolerant nation and have a superb sense of humour, and there is plenty of compassion for asylum seekers in distress. We do not, however, like to be made fools of or to be lied to. We do not like immigrants to be treated better than us. We do not like thousands of military-age young men cynically coming here to claim benefits, get their teeth fixed, update their social media profile, buy new trainers, ogle and harass our wives and daughters, and then laugh at us for being a soft touch.

We do not like politicians like Rishi Sunak telling us in early 2024 that many thousands of asylum seekers would be shipped off to Rwanda each year when he knew from the Home Office that the maximum that could go would be 3,000 over five years. We do not like politicians like Kier Starmer telling us that he would bring down the backlog of asylum seekers without telling us he planned to give them an amnesty and let them become citizens, including those who could be terrorists and intend to do us harm.

I went on to stand against Michael Howard in Folkestone on a platform of no immigration and the castration of paedophiles. I formed my own political party, the 'Get Britain Back Party', a phrase we have heard many times since then from Nigel Farage and others. I had no doubts. I fully expected to have to sleep with my researcher, to fiddle my election expenses and spend my evenings on Clapham Common watching badgers.

In the event, as an independent, I stood no chance and polled slightly less than the Raving Loony Party, but I gave the Conservatives a sufficient shock that they changed their immigration policy during the campaign. They took out a full-page advert in the Telegraph, saying they would limit immigration after the election. They did not, of course, do so during the 14 years when they were in power, and the public booted them out in 2024.

TORIES TAKE POTTS' SHOT

IT can be no coincidence that a week after right-wing Rodney Hylton-Potts won ITV's Vote For Me by proposing a halt to immigration, Michael Howard chose to put the issue at the front of his election campaign.

Viewers, a stunned Tory party realised, had voted overwhelmingly not for this vile individual but for his message. I know from the bucketload of letters I receive from readers that the majority welcome genuine refugees who keep our cities going and contribute so much to public services.

What the British public can't stomach is illegal immigrants, bogus asylum seekers, spongers, organised people smuggling, increased street crime perpetrated by foreign gangs, fudged immigration figures, an appalling lack of border control, and the arrogance of a government which refuses to even debate this crucial issue on the basis it may be "racist".

VILE: Right wing Rod Potts

Hylton-Potts will not go down in the history books as a politician. But he might make a footnote as the man who dared put his head over the parapet to fire the first shot.

The open-door policy is with us to this day. Mine was a wake-up call in 2005, but few listened. In any view, Britain is overcrowded, but if you point it out, there are howls and accusations of racism. This is absolute rubbish. They say today that for years, the British public has implored politicians to bring down the rate of immigration, but that is not the case. The public has been asleep at the wheel. Our island home, once so wonderful, is horribly overcrowded. Heavy traffic, crowds, waiting lists at GPs, hospitals, for housing and schools and tens of thousands who do not even like our way of life. This is such a shame, and nobody voted for it.

If you want a laugh, click on YouTube: 'Vote for me Rodney Hylton-Potts'. There are two short 10-minute clips, which I think you might like. Look out for Maud and the bricks!

https://www.youtube.com/watch?v=aIhrUK3Fhwg

https://www.youtube.com/watch?v=3D-7YBfHgbY

FOOTNOTE

Here is an article I wrote for the Daily Mail in 2005 that might resonate today:

The Gulf

Do we get the politicians we deserve? You bet we do, and in spades. With voter apathy at its highest since World War One and less than half the young voting, we do indeed get and deserve a motley crew.

There have been, of course, obvious exceptions: Tony Benn, Bob Marshall-Andrews, Dennis Skinner. The few tough-minded independent MPs who never mindlessly toed the party line.

But look at the rest. Would you employ most of them, or any of them, to run your business while you took a month or two off? Would you buy a second-hand car from them?

Once every five years, they come to call, knocking on our doors, kissing our babies and asking for money for their causes. Between elections, we are ignored at best and, it seems, sometimes even disliked for being a nuisance.

But it gets worse. We all know Tony Blair will get back in this May. With a reduced majority, no doubt, but he will get back in. Senior Tories are said to admit as much in private.

We are, therefore, going to get one of the most distrusted men in Britain at the helm for another five years. Can you imagine what this discredited, control-obsessed politician will inflict on the British people over the next five years to ensure his place in history?

Politicians (a so-called "profession") have an approval rating of 14%, even below car dealers and estate agents. Ministers have an even lower rating of 11%, and yet, for five more years, we will be led by one of the worst of all. He can organise (or rig) as many enquiries as he likes. We all know about the infamous, sexed-up 45-minute dossier. We can argue whitewash, enquiries and genuine mistakes, but what everybody knows deep in their hearts is that when Blair said it, it was designed to push us into a war and mislead us with false information. We feel it in our gut, and that is not a bad thing when considering politics. Blair has even stitched up his best mate, Gordon Brown.

And then there is religion. Many regret it, but churchgoing is at an all-time low in the UK. But not with politicians. Many politicians seem to go to church far more than any other families, but always with a camera in hand. Cynical? You bet, but they made us so. But Blair is worse. He has a slight maniacal glint of religious fervour in his eye, which is deeply worrying.

But things cannot be that bad, you say. After all, we live in a democracy, and all our MPs are elected to do what we voted for. Wrong again. Blair himself is even more cynical about democracy than you or even I could ever be. In the 2003-04 session, he only bothered to vote 6% of the time - the worst Commons voting record of any modern prime minister. He treats our democratic Parliament with the same contempt that he treats us, the electorate. If Blair couldn't care less about voting, why should we? No wonder we're cynical about politicians.

Then take the pound. There are arguments by people much cleverer than I, with access to Treasury models I can never comprehend. Deep in the heart of every Briton, however, is the feeling, the knowledge, that to give up the pound would be madness and no price for economic growth would be worth giving up our sovereignty. Our pensioners fought two world wars to keep our nation free. To even consider giving up our pound would be a betrayal. But the politicians say there will be a referendum. We have all heard it before. As sure as night follows day, if we stay in Europe, we will join the euro and ditch the pound at some future date, and future generations will never forgive us.

Take Europe, the biggest con trick in politics since Hitler invaded Czechoslovakia. We joined a free trade zone to promote jobs and prosperity. We now have a hugely enlarged ramshackle group of nations generally much poorer than we are, led by the Teutonic partnership (ironic that) of Germany and France. This can only lead to a European Super State, a Europe run by faceless, un-elected bureaucrats with subsidies and fraud. We never voted for it, but we've got it.

Take immigration. Britain is full. That is not a racist remark - I hate racism. But what do our politicians say? They are terrified of actually telling the truth. They are terrified of saying that when the Daily Mail publishes an article about Neasden in London, where 63 houses are in a street, of which 58 are occupied by ethnic minorities, it is worrying because they might be accused of being racist. The British are a tolerant people without peer. That is one of the things that has made us great. Over centuries, we have had Anglo-Saxons, Normans, Germans, French, Irish, Dutch and, latterly, the New Commonwealth and Australians and New Zealanders forging a caring and tolerant society. What everybody knows (but the politicians will not say) is that if there is one significant large group, it is unsettling. This is not racist. The same would apply if there was a large group of Boris Johnson lookalikes! We, the ordinary public, say it, but politicians will not reflect it. That is the gulf.

Drugs. There is this mealy-mouthed nonsense about whether politicians inhaled a joint at university. Marijuana and cannabis are widely used drugs, and politicians use them. So do judges, accountants, lawyers, doctors and bank managers. So do bus drivers, policemen (mainly off-duty) and mini-cab drivers. Some even take the odd line of cocaine, as we have seen again and again. But what do we find? We have this absolute hypocrisy of politicians who take drugs, who allow their houses to be used for drugs and go to dinner parties where drugs are taken, prattling on about the evil of drugs when they do not believe a word of it, as it applies to them. I am old enough to remember the days when being a politician was a public service. You went into it because - just like other people in our society who give blood, volunteer for good causes, or donate to charity - you believed in giving the community something back. Today, of course, it's every man for himself. People go into politics as a 'career' - think of all those directorships, those two Jags (at least), all that oiling and greasing of palm. Bad luck if you forget to sign the Register of Members' Interests, of course.

But even then, when they get caught out, they don't accept responsibility. For people who are supposed to set an example, they're lousy role models. Remember Mad Cow Disease? They lied, and people died, but no one accepted the blame. Remember the Dome? They blew £1 billion of public money - and no one accepted responsibility. And don't get me started on the Iraq war and the endless prevarications of Messrs. Blair and Hoon.

So what's the solution? A start might be to elect someone of the ilk of Martin Bell, who did such a great job having overturned Neil

Hamilton. As an independent MP not vetted by a party machine, he stood against sleaze.

The Dutch politician Pym Fortuyn dramatically showed the changes that can be made when a politician says what people are reluctant to say out loud or only say in private. In Great Britain, people are no longer allowed to make discriminatory remarks or say what they think, if not 'politically correct'. Focussing on a small number of specific and radical changes, stated in plain English without the nauseating political spin the main parties give, would enable even a sole independent MP to push the government of the day to give people what they actually want.

Don't believe the politicians when they tell us that the only choice is between left or right. Don't believe them when they say that a vote for an independent candidate is a vote wasted. And don't believe Tony Blair when he tries to con us and then does not bother to vote himself.

Every vote counts. Every person in this great nation of ours counts. If we don't vote, then nothing will change. But if we do, then we may just begin to get the kind of government that we actually want, not what is presently stuffed down our throats.

Goosing

Lawyers are bound by confidentiality and cannot reveal the secrets of their cases without a client's consent, which is rarely forthcoming. An exception, however, is Fraser Marr, a case I was instructed on in 1989. It appears in the Law Reports and is a leading appeal case on a demonstration in court and snide remarks from prosecution-minded judges. So, I am allowed to tell you about this case with the names and intimate details.

Fraser Marr was 27 and an art dealer with no care in the world. His glamorous girlfriend, Laura Luxton, aged 21 (at that time, all blonde girls seemed to be called Laura or Fiona), also worked in Mayfair, near the art gallery where he was a trainee dealer.

On 19 September 1989, he had an hour for lunch and, as usual, would walk up Regent Street, with its familiar, attractive crescent of upmarket shops and shoppers. He walked around Mayfair to get some exercise. He also wanted to get some theatre tickets and intended to buy the best seats to impress his girlfriend.

It was a sunny autumn day, and he could not believe his luck. His day was complete. Walking in front of him, swaying rather attractively on the pavement in jodhpurs and a jacket, was his lovely, shapely Laura, her long, shiny hair swinging tantalisingly from side to side.

Now, dear reader, I must ask you this: what is 'Goosing'? Do you know? Think about it - although perhaps not for too long, or you might be arrested by the thought police or the #MeToo movement.

To the uninitiated, 'Goosing' takes place when a man (usually) with a straight arm (notice the arm must be straight) gently moves or even drives his arm in an upwards motion between a girl's buttocks before traditionally crying ", *Ooh!*" or "*Gotya*!" The hand is curled between the legs, mimicking the shape of the goose's neck. Practice it. It is OK to do it at home. Indeed, it should only be done behind closed doors.

With someone you know, it is harmless, although possibly irritating, fun. Fraser decided he would surprise Laura with a well-practised 'goose'.

He caught her up with a quickening of his step and, with his straight arm, goosed her between the legs, his hand moving upwards between her tantalisingly attractive and pert buttocks. Laura stopped, turned around, and glared.

It was not her! He had just assaulted a complete stranger, a girl aged 19. A more mature man would have apologised profusely, explained how like his girlfriend she was and offered to buy her some flowers. A grovelling apology would have been called for and probably accepted.

But Fraser was not that experienced. He panicked. He turned and ran down Regent Street as fast as he could with the lookalike shouting, "*Come back*". She chased him and was joined by a public-minded man, but he was too fast for them.

He turned left into a side street, with several people shouting after him, but he ran faster. It was then that his luck changed for the worse. On the corner was a Constable Johnson in plain clothes, watching nothing in particular, when he saw Fraser running and heard the shouts. Unfortunately for Fraser, he turned out to be the

Harringay Police Sprint Champion. He caught up with Fraser, grabbed his jacket and brought him down to his knees. Fraser was noted to have said, "*I've done nothing. Please let me go.*" The policeman frogmarched him back to the victim, who stated in front of Fraser what had happened. The policeman then cautioned and arrested Fraser, and he was taken to the police station.

When formally interviewed under caution, he said he thought the girl he had touched was his girlfriend Laura, who resembled the stranger. He said, untruthfully, that he had decided to catch up with her and, as he passed her, intended to turn, face her, walk backwards for a moment and say hello. He reached out, but at the moment he realised it was not Laura, it was too late. The momentum of his arm in the curling goosing motion hit her vaginal area. Because the girl looked very upset, he panicked and ran away. He did not say he intended to 'goose' Laura and did himself no favours during the interview.

As you will see elsewhere in this book (see chapter 14), I never allow my clients to answer police questions in police interviews. Unfortunately for Fraser, he was assigned a free legal aid 'duty' solicitor and dug a deeper hole for himself. Legal aid solicitors are often compassionate, decent people but on terrible legal aid pay, overworked, and do not have the same time to devote to a case as a private solicitor. It is a third-class service. The prisons are full of people who were on legal aid.

He began to change his story in a way he thought would help him. It did not. Thus, it came about that he was charged with indecent assault, a Court date was fixed, and he became my client. He stressed he did not want his boss to find out, as if that happened, he would certainly be sacked.

I instructed Robert Grey, a clever, attractive and amusing barrister who specialised in sex and drug cases. I sat behind Robert. This will become important.

In the witness box, Fraser told his story, again with subtle differences he thought would help his case. He would have done much better to stick to the truth, as I had told him.

He said it had been lunchtime. He was on his way to get some tickets for the theatre. Because he thought he saw his girlfriend Laura Luxton walking in front of him, he decided to catch up with her. It was his intention to pass her by and then, whilst facing her, walk backwards and exchange a few words before he continued on his way. When he drew alongside her, just as he was about to turn to face her, he suddenly realised it was not Laura Luxton at all. He told the court that at that very moment, he happened to be on the curb and lost his footing. In order to regain his balance, he reached out with his right hand, and his hand accidentally went between the girl's thighs. He said he did not squeeze her private parts. As he withdrew his hand, it did press against them, which may have felt like a squeeze to her. He was very embarrassed and decided it was best to leave rapidly and not to make matters any worse. Hence, the running away.

The defence called his girlfriend, Laura, to give evidence in the witness box. There was a resemblance in the hairstyle between her and the stranger, but there was a difference in their heights and in their body shape: the stranger was much taller and bustier than Laura. So was Fraser really mistaken, or was he guilty of what the judge called a "*furtive little crime*" in a snide aside to the jury?

During the course of cross-examination by the barrister for the police, Fraser was asked to step down from the witness box and to give a demonstration of how he said the incident had taken place. The judge decided that the jury would need a live demonstration to see how easy it would be for Fraser to have made this mistake. The case turned on whether a man's action whilst '*goosing*' with his arm in an upward trajectory cannot be stopped. The arm comes into contact with the girl's clothing but drives upwards (whilst trying this at home, it is more fun when the girl wears a skirt). Was there a moment the jury had to decide when Fraser went ahead anyway, or was it a genuine mistake?

There is a common misconception about juries. People think that they are 12 unemployed scroungers who are only doing jury duty because they received a letter and it was raining, so they can get £68 a day and a hot lunch and sit there nodding off and playing video games on their phones. Nothing could be further from the truth. Juries take their duties extremely seriously and can see and smell dishonesty, just as you and I can in real life.

When the time came for re-examination, the judge refused to allow Robert Grey to adopt the demonstration procedure he had asked for. Mischievously, Robert had asked that it might be done using a female model. Smiles crept over the faces of the jurors and barristers.

Hearing the suggestion of using a female model to demonstrate the '*goosing*' episode, the judge completely lost it: he said that his court was a Court of Law, not a circus. He also pointed out, to some laughter, that there was no female on the defence legal team to assist in the demo. This resulted in stage whispers and jokes about a skirt being brought in and worn by me. Robert concluded that the judge might have had a sense of humour failure.

The judge ruled against allowing the demonstration argument and, in summing up, as I have said, referred to a "*furtive little crime*". Fraser was convicted. The judge sentenced him to 21 days in jail, despite the fact that he had no previous convictions and lots of excellent character references, and ordered him to pay the prosecution costs of £475.

Robert Gray said he was going to appeal, and fortunately, the judge granted Fraser bail pending the appeal. He appealed to the Court of Appeal and was successful. The case is R v. Marr (Fraser) 90 CRIM Criminal Appeals on page 154. It is in the Appendix. The Lord Chief Justice in the Court of Appeal ruled that the judge should have allowed the demonstration, and this has become a leading case in demonstrations. The judge said, "*The appellant complains that the learned judge conducted the case in such a way that it was not, to put it bluntly, given a fair run. However distasteful the offence, however repulsive the defendant, however laughable his defence, he is entitled to a fair trial.*"

You will recall that Fraser had made it clear to me that he did not want any publicity because if his boss found out, he would be fired. Fraser's conviction was set aside, but not only did he fail to avoid publicity, but he was in every newspaper and all over every law report, and his name is now synonymous with '*goosing*' and the law on whether juries should see a demonstration.

You win some, you lose some.

I highly recommend you try your own ‘goosing’ demonstration at home. If you do, you can form your own opinion about whether Fraser did it.

The Human Lie Detector

A new client called John came into my office. He was about 50, balding, nervous and seemed keen to end the meeting quickly. He told his story. He had been married for over 20 years. He wanted to save his marriage, but there were major problems at home.

He said that he loved his wife very much, but she was ill. She masturbated literally all day and every day, often standing on the kitchen table in their house, and sometimes men would gather in the street to see her when she pulled up her skirt.

He had pleaded with her to stop. He had spoken to her brother, saying how worried he was about her mental health, but the brother said that John was disgusting, that he did not believe a word of it and that he had a foul mouth and should shut up.

All John wanted to do was to persuade the brother that what he was telling him was the truth and, therefore, he wanted to know how much a lie detector test would be.

I did not know but said I would find out, and I did, there and then, and came back into the meeting room with the answer: about £900.00 plus VAT.

He thanked me warmly and said he could not afford that and did I owe him anything. I said, *"No,"* and he got up to leave. Just before he left, however, I said, "*Please sit down, I have an idea".*

I said that for a much cheaper fee, I had a suggestion which might appeal to him. One of the lawyers here could listen to his story and decide whether he was telling the truth. It would be much cheaper than the lie detector test. She worked with me, but she would do him no favours and would swear an Affidavit, saying whether or not she believed him. If she did believe him, he could show that Affidavit to the brother.

He said that was absolutely brilliant, paid the fee, and Maud joined the meeting. Maud, my wife, is a skilled and experienced adviser with a very good feel and nose for bullshit.

I took him through his story, and Maud made notes on a yellow legal pad. When he got to the part about his wife standing on the kitchen table exposing herself to the street, with men watching her whilst she was masturbating, I asked him where he had been at that time. He said he was standing in the hall.

Question: "*Was there a door between the hall and the kitchen*?"

Answer: "*Yes.*"

Question: "*Was the door open or closed?"*

Answer: "*Closed."*

Question: "*How did you know she was masturbating if the door was closed*?"

Answer: "*The noises she made."*

I glanced at Maud at this point, and she was beginning to struggle to contain her mirth. She could see what was coming. She could see where I was going, and there was no escape.

Question: "*Can you please describe for Mrs Bergvelt the noise that your wife made when masturbating?"*

Yes, said John, and made a funny "*mmmm/ohohoh/mmmmm*" murmuring sound.

At this point, Maud lost it completely, hoping I would not look at her, and rushed off to contain her explosion of laughter, which I could hear from next door. She eventually composed herself and returned to the meeting and heard John's story out.

She then swore an Affidavit saying she believed him, which she did, and we discovered later he had shown it to the brother, and it had worked. After reading the Affidavit, the brother believed him and made sure that his sister received help.

So here you have another example of lateral and light-hearted thinking producing a brilliant result for a client and possibly saving a marriage. John's, that is, not mine.

That's Life

It was a cold Sunday evening in February 1977, and I was in bed at home in St George's Hill, Weybridge. I was in bed early as I had a gruelling week's work ahead.

The TV was on in the bedroom. Few people had a TV there in those days. I was a partner in a solicitors' firm called Outred and Co. Outred was the family name of my then-wife, and her brother was my partner. Outred is an old Kent name that features in the Domesday book. Another long, hard-working week lay ahead. I was reading the Sunday papers before nodding off when I heard my name on the TV.

The show was BBC's 'That's Life' with Esther Rantzen.

I had a client called Mr Bernard Ealey, to whom I had sent a bill for £41.04. I had deducted that amount from the sale proceeds of his house, but I had made a mistake and thought he still owed it, so I issued a summons in Court for him to pay me, which was wrong because he had already paid me.

When this came to light, I apologised and dropped the case. However, Mr Ealey was still not happy, and he contacted 'That's Life', an investigative journalism programme. Esther Rantzen was its popular presenter, who went on to do great work with Childline, a children's charity, and to campaign for the right to choose assisted dying. Later in life, I recall children threatening their parents with a call to Esther Rantzen's Childline if they thought they were being unfairly disciplined.

A week earlier, a BBC journalist from the show phoned me to ask if I could discuss the case, and I said I could if Mr Ealey gave permission, which he did. I then asked them who would pay for my time talking to them.

They said that it was called investigative journalism and that nobody charged for it. I saw things differently, so I sent That's Life a bill for my time, which came to £15.12, including VAT, and forgot about it until that Sunday evening.

That is how my name came to be on TV, not least because the piece ended with the words, "*We are sending his bill to the Law Society to see if it is fair and reasonable. Mind you, judging by the car Mr Rodney Hylton-Potts has and drives; he will not really mind either way.*"

The camera then panned up the grill of my Rolls Royce and then down to the number plate, RHP11.

It is said that no publicity is bad publicity. Certainly, this was very good for my business and attracted significant attention, especially when I wrote to Esther Rantzen saying I was "free" after the show! (see the Letter and Law Society certificate below).

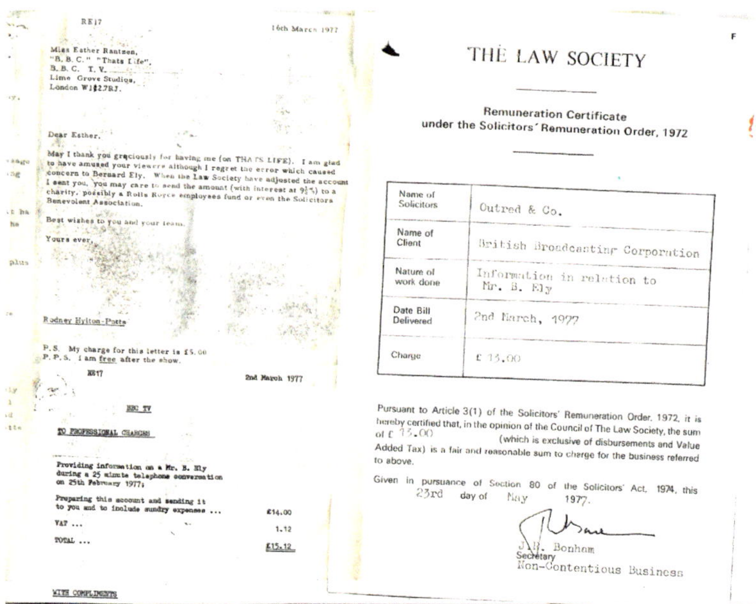

RE17

16th March 1977

Miss Esther Rantzen,
"B. B. C." "Thats Life",
B. B. C. T. V.
Lime Grove Studios,
London W12 7RJ.

Dear Esther,

May I thank you graciously for having me (on THATS LIFE). I am glad to have amused your viewers although I regret the error which caused concern to Bernard Ely. When the Law Society have adjusted the account I sent you, you may care to send the amount (with interest at 9½%) to a charity, possibly a Rolls Royce employees fund or even the Solicitors Benevolent Association.

Best wishes to you and your team.

Yours ever,

Rodney Hylton-Potts

P.S. My charge for this letter is £5.00
P.P.S. I am free after the show.

RE17

2nd March 1977

BBC TV

TO PROFESSIONAL CHARGES

Providing information on a Mr. B. Ely during a 25 minute telephone conversation on 25th February 1977;

Preparing this account and sending it to you and to include sundry expenses ... £14.00

VAT ... 1.12

TOTAL ... £15.12

WITH COMPLIMENTS

THE LAW SOCIETY

Remuneration Certificate
under the Solicitors' Remuneration Order, 1972

Name of Solicitors	Outred & Co.
Name of Client	British Broadcasting Corporation
Nature of work done	Information in relation to Mr. B. Ely
Date Bill Delivered	2nd March, 1977
Charge	£ 13.00

Pursuant to Article 3(1) of the Solicitors' Remuneration Order, 1972, it is hereby certified that, in the opinion of the Council of The Law Society, the sum of £ 13.00 (which is exclusive of disbursements and Value Added Tax) is a fair and reasonable sum to charge for the business referred to above.

Given in pursuance of Section 80 of the Solicitors' Act, 1974, this 23rd day of May 1977.

J. R. Bonham
Secretary
Non-Contentious Business

Unlike You, He Is 20!

Nick was 20 years old, a university student who liked rugby, partying, and girls. Good for him. He was handsome, if slightly crumpled and clever. People who met him liked him at once, and older people quietly thought they would love a son, or son-in-law, like him.

He and a group of male and female student friends, all aged around 20, went to Twickenham to watch the rugby. He is not sure how much he drank. Some guesstimated during the day that he had drunk fourteen pints, but, whatever the truth, he had drunk steadily all morning, during the match and afterwards.

He returned to Chelsea with his mates, and they had a kebab in a café, then went back to someone's house. He was as horny as hell and had his eye on a girl in the group, whom I shall now refer to as 'the target'.

With more drinks inside him at the house (no drugs as far as I could determine), Nick saw his chance as he saw the target enter a bedroom. Seizing the opportunity, he waited a few moments and followed her into the room. He was too late. A friend of his had arrived first and was already in bed with the target. He began to watch them. They told him to get out and behave himself, and to his credit, he did, going back outside the bedroom door.

He then masturbated.

Following this, he then drank some more and may have fallen asleep. Either way, at some later point, he decided to try his luck again and entered the bedroom to find 'the target' still there, but this time alone.

She was lying face down with her bed touching the wall, in the well-known spoon position, her legs slightly bent in a type of foetal position.

Stripping off and seeing that she was asleep, he rubbed up against her and became erect. She groaned. He became more and more excited and then became harder and harder and pushed his penis gently inside her bottom. Later on, he could not remember doing this, and he was probably trying to find her vagina. At this point, she woke up and pushed him away, shouting. He left at once, apologetic and ashamed, or that is how he remembered it. The truth was, he was still very drunk. The girl was not hurt or cut, nor did she bleed.

It sounds like a rather grubby but typical teenage evening gone wrong. Some ladies I have told this story to think it is nothing, just a clumsy teenage slip-up. Others say it is a clear-cut anal rape, being just as bad as vaginal rape, and should be treated as seriously. What do you think?

The Police took a second view when the girl complained, and five weeks later, Nick was arrested at his university by five policemen, including one carrying a firearm.

His parents contacted me to represent him. My wife, Maud, is from the Netherlands and an integral part of the firm. In this case, her role was to go to the Police Station to take down details of everything that had happened that evening and report back to me.

She came back with the story I outlined above. I carefully listened to her summary of the events as told to her by Nick. I said to her I did not mind in the least because you are a woman, but did you not ask him whether his masturbation came to a conclusion (did he climax?)? The point I was making was that if he had, he would not have been horny again, and it would have been far less likely for him to have gone back with sex in mind a couple of hours later.

She turned to me and said: "*Now listen carefully. I will say this only once. Two things. Firstly, never tell me how to do my job, and, secondly, you are forgetting something. Unlike you, he is 20."* Collapse of another stout party, so to speak

His parents were keen that he should get bail, and I could see no problem until the prosecutor told the magistrates an extraordinary story. In the period between that fateful night and his being arrested, he had wanted to express his apology to the girl, so he had sent her a message saying, "*I have identified somebody who will beat me up and video me. Would that be sufficient*?"

In other words, he was genuinely offering to arrange to have himself beaten up sufficiently badly for there to be visible marks so that he could send that to the girl in the hope that she would take no further action and would forgive him. This latest development was news to me and to his parents. This was the prosecution summary:

The victim said [illegible] and [illegible] could sleep in the lounge and set up the sofa bed for them. The victim and [illegible] went to her bedroom and had consensual sex. While they were having sex the suspect came in and began to watch them. He was asked to leave. The victim and [illegible] fell asleep. The victim then stated that she was woken up because someone was having anal sex with her. She turned around and the suspect was holding her waist. She could feel his penis inside her. She pushed him away and asked him what he was doing. The suspect said he was sorry.

The suspect subsequently left the room and the victim eventually went to sleep because she didn't know what to do about what had just happened. She woke up in the morning and told [illegible] what happened. [illegible] confronted the suspect and asked if he had raped [illegible]. He said he did not remember anything.

On 7th November 2006 the suspect wrote a letter to the victim apologising about his actions. The suspect then called the victim on 14th November 2006. On 5th December 2006 the victim received text messages from the suspect. The suspect continued to apologise and say sorry for his actions. The suspect continued to send text messages to the victim asking for forgiveness and stated he was disgusted at what he had done. He asked if it could all be sorted out privately.

The magistrates were not impressed and denied him bail. His parents ran out of money at that point and probably 'went Legal Aid'. Legal Aid solicitors can be dedicated and passionate, and some are skilful, but they do not have time to devote to such cases. I heard that he went to jail for five years and that his life and future career were ruined. I am pretty sure I could have kept him out of jail or even got him an acquittal.

I shall never personally forget, however, the stinging words, "*Unlike you, he is 20!*".

A SEXUAL CONSENT FORM

Nick's case and many others gave me an idea. In the 70s, 80s and 90s, men regularly tried to get girls into bed using alcohol as a tool. Those days have gone since the #MeToo movement. Now informed consent is essential, and without it, a man can get into very serious trouble, including allegations of rape.

Although unromantic, I have drafted a sexual contract to be produced in the bar or swiped right on Tinder before the couple goes somewhere private. See what you think. It may look pretty clinical, even horrible, but it may become more accepted than you think.

Sexual Consent Form & Right of Privacy Agreement

I, ________________________________of, ________________________________ hereby declare under penalty of perjury that I am over 16 years old.

I further declare that this agreement is of my own free will and that neither I nor anyone near or dear to me has been threatened with harm or embarrassment.

Both parties agree that this is a private agreement not to be disclosed to third parties except in case of an accusation of sexual misconduct by the agreeing party. If he/she shows or makes public this agreement without accusation of sexual misconduct, it is agreed that he/she will be liable for damages for invasion of privacy.

By initialling, _____ I agree to engage in all or some of the following consensual acts below:

- *Sexual fondling and kissing*
- *Oral sex (mutual)*
- *Oral sex (unilateral) by ______________________ only*
- *Sexual intercourse (with a condom at all times) (DELETE IF CONDOM NOT A REQUIREMENT)*

Other consensual sexual conduct to be specified:

____
____

____
____

____
____

____
____

I further declare that I am at this time not under the influence of alcohol, drugs or medication and agree to engage in consensual sex with:

____

At this time, I do not intend to change my mind before the sex act or acts are over, and this agreement shall continue without a time limit. If I wish to change my mind, I will put it in writing, including text or e-mail to the other party.

Signed: ______________________________ *Date:* ______________________________

Signed: ______________________________ *Date:* _________________________________

Disclaimer: Check with your lawyer before entering into any agreement.

White Van Woman

Guy liked rugby and drinking and, in 2014, just like Nick in the last chapter, he went to Twickenham but, unlike Nick, he drove his car. On the way back to London, the Police stopped him, and he was found to be four times over the legal limit on a breathalyser test. Four times over the limit is incredibly serious and means that he was paralytic behind the wheel, not just tipsy. Magistrates take a very serious view, and prison was a real possibility.

His lawyer told him he would go to prison, probably for six months. The sentence would not be suspended. He would be sent straight from Court to Brixton. Guy could not face the prospect, so he jumped bail, packed his case and his passport and went to live in China.

Guy was an engaging fellow, aged 60, who dabbled in property and had a ready smile. He left behind his wife, Ciaji, who was Chinese, twenty years younger, pretty and slim. He left her with no real explanation and no money. He was not very nice to her. She owned her house but had no income. If a woman in those circumstances has no other training or occupation and needs to put food on the table, would you criticise her for turning to prostitution? Anyway, that is what she did, but out of respect for Guy, even though he had behaved so badly, she did not invite her clients into the house and marital bed.

Instead, she acquired a white Ford Transit van, which she parked in the drive.

The mind boggles to think what it was like on the inside, but it worked well enough. Indeed, it had red curtains, music, a double bed and numerous sex toys.

About five years later, Guy contacted me. As with most of my new clients, I had been recommended. He said he wanted to face the music and come home, and what could I do for him? I told him that I could almost certainly arrange for him not to be hauled off the plane in handcuffs but to get the police to 'do it the nice way'. He would meet the Police at the immigration gate at City Airport, where they would quietly take him off to avoid embarrassment. I said I could not keep him out of jail for jumping bail and that he might have to serve three months, plus a further six months for the original drink-driving offence. The game was up.

He was resigned to this and, by arrangement, he flew into City Airport, the Police having agreed to meet and arrest him at the gate and take him to Court. Crucially, the Police agreed to arrest him at the immigration gate and not take him off the plane upon landing.

I spoke to Ciaji, who said she would bring the deeds of her house to Court to support the application for bail, pending a sentencing hearing. One of my paralegals and Ciaji were at the immigration gate to meet him and to say hello prior to him being whisked away. He texted me from the plane to say all was well and that nobody had hauled him off the plane. He was fully expecting to spend his first night in jail because I told him that, despite the house deeds, he would not get bail and would not be going home.

After jumping bail back in 2014, no magistrate was going to set him loose, as I told his wife, but she insisted on bringing the house deeds to support a bail application anyway.
When he came through immigration, however, there was no sign of any police at all. My paralegal had to hunt down a random policeman at the airport to get them to arrest him. At 2.00 pm in the local Court, the Crown Prosecution Service were clearly embarrassed by their cock up and said that they would not proceed further, saying they had lost the file.

I know this was not true because we had had discussions about the case, but clearly, they did not want it to get out that he had walked, unimpeded and unchecked, through immigration when on a wanted list. The same list is used to track Islamic terrorists and IRA bomb suspects. The Daily Mail would have had a field day.

Relieved and delighted with me, he turned to his wife, Ciaji and said, "*Let's go home*". She blustered. She needed time to think. She urged him to celebrate with my paralegal or go and see me at my office in Fulham and come home later.

Why? Parked in the drive was the white van that she had not expected to have to move just yet. He seemed puzzled by what she said, but she managed to buy enough time to move it. He knew exactly what she was up to, however, and was silently hugely amused.

Unbeknown to her, he had planned to divorce her all along and knew the white van was there, and so did I. Before he came back to England, he had asked me to get a private detective to check her out. The white van and the use she put it to was easily discovered. I expect the private detective I instructed felt it was his duty to become a client!

So the wife's loyalty in sticking up for him, putting up the deeds of her house for bail and meeting him at the airport was met with a divorce and a poor financial settlement.

No good deed goes unpunished.

From Zero To Hero

In 1999, I came out of prison, divorced (no, my wife did not wait), not allowed to see our children and with a very uncertain future. I had to start again with nothing. My ex-wife took everything.

I did something that nobody else has ever successfully done, which is to take on solicitors head-on as a competitor, providing legal consultancy services often for fixed fees. Not being bound by the Solicitors Regulation Authority's outdated rules, I could do anything I liked. If somebody owed money to a client, I could ring them up or descend on them in a restaurant or club and tell them to pay up and not eat and drink my client's money away.

I was a wild card, a maverick; I enjoyed it and got plenty of work from people who could well have afforded a top firm of solicitors.

Some people sought me out because they thought I was going to be a bent lawyer to help them in some criminal scheme. They were to be disappointed, but my lateral thinking appealed to many. If a client of mine had a cut-glass, posh aristocratic accent, that could be of help in all sorts of circumstances, such as being misunderstood by a train guard over a missing first-class ticket. If my client was black or came from an Asian minority, I could play upon the fear that people, including the police and employers, have of being accused of being racist.

If I did not know enough of a particular area of the Law, I would readily ask my opponent, who could be the Crown Prosecution Service, a fraud investigator or a General Medical Counsel lawyer, to help me out, and I invariably received huge courtesy and lots of tips so I could basically do anything, and I did. Judges got to know me. My name is unusual. The only aggravation I ever got was from solicitors on the other side, who sometimes complained I was treading on their toes. Invariably, this was when their client had a weak case, and they had nothing better to say. Most recognised that I was entitled to earn my living.

How have I done so well? By not accepting anything and challenging everything. For example, we have all seen it on TV. The police arrest somebody, and they are fingerprinted, have their DNA taken and placed in a cell, and sometimes see a doctor. They are then told that they will be interviewed in an interview room.

An interview can be frightening and intimidating, and it is intended to be. You are given the caution, and it is on tape under the Police and Civil Evidence Act. Fraud investigators use technology to analyse your voice for signs of stress. This can then be interpreted as guilt. Thousands of claimants are caught each year using this technique, also used for telephone interviews.

At a face-to-face interview, under caution, they thrust documents at you without warning and try to catch you out. A prosecution is far more likely if they think you are not being 100% straight with them.

A suspect will go into the interview room, usually with a Legal Aid duty solicitor, called by the police, who sits in on the interview. You have seen it many times. Very often, the accused says "*No comment*" over and over. Saying "*No comment*" in an interview is a disaster, especially when said repeatedly. Judges hate it. Jurors hate it. They want to hear the version from the suspect. Try this:

"Were you in Mary's house on Sunday?" "*No comment.*"

"Did you know she owned a valuable brooch?" "*No comment.*"

"Were you aware that she found the brooch was missing?" "*No comment.*"

"Did you, in fact, take the brooch?" "*No comment.*"

Complete disaster.

Lie detector voice tests trap 4,000 fraudsters

By **Sam Greenhill**

A LIE detector test trapped nearly 4,000 benefit cheats in just four months.

The offenders were picking up council tax discounts worth £1.4million by falsely claiming they lived alone.

But they were caught out by technology that analyses phone calls for signs of stress in the speaker's voice.

Southwark council in South London used the system to check on 53,000 households claiming the 25 per cent council tax discount.

It found that in approximately one in 13 cases, the discount was being wrongly claimed.

A council spokesman said: 'We are very pleased with the results. Between July and November, we have removed 3,851 people from the list of those claiming the discount.

'It has resulted in additional bills of £1.4million of council tax which is payable.'

The voice risk analysis system works by analysing the pitch of callers' voices when they are asked questions by council officials.

'Very pleased with the results'

If the system suspects a lie is being told, a beep sounds in the operator's ear. Once alerted, the operator is trained to begin asking questions that may uncover the truth.

It can lead to a full investigation into claims for housing benefit, council tax, income support and jobseeker's allowance. Claimants are warned in advance that the phone call is being 'recorded and monitored for the detection of fraud'.

Anyone who refuses to take part in the call is likely to be visited in person for an assessment of their claim.

It is not the first time lie detectors have been used by councils. Former work and pensions secretary John Hutton ordered a pilot study four years ago in which 24 local authorities tested the concept.

Two years ago, however, the Government abandoned the detector tests saying they were unreliable.

An academic study also raised doubts by suggesting the technology was little better than 'astronomy' at detecting fraud.

Insurance companies similar systems to catch fraudsters.

A Southwark spokesman said claimants who did not speak English as their first language or had hearing or cognitive problems were exempt from the voice checks.

Richard Livingstone, the council's cabinet member for finance and resources, said: 'We are taking a tough stance against fraud.

'Any resident found making a false claim will be fully investigated and the necessary action taken.'

A spokesman for Capita – the private firm contracted by Southwark to carry out the checks – said it preferred not to describe it as a lie detector test, insisting it used the voice checking system together with 'behavioural analysis by trained operators'.

He insisted: 'The technology is not used in isolation.'

A spokesman for London Councils said he did not know of any other authorities in the capital using the system.

A similar response was given by a spokesman for the Local Government Association, which represents 423 authorities across Britain.

Harrow Council has used the voice analysis system to check on housing benefit and council tax benefit claims.

A spokesman for the authority said: 'We did try this technology but stopped using it three years ago.'

s.greenhill@dailymail.co.uk

I went back to basics. By what legal right do the police say you have to go into the interview room at all? If ever a client of mine is arrested and placed in a cell, he is told by me to hold his nerve and keep his mouth shut. The police have no power to make you even go into the interview room. But even if you are frogmarched to an interview room (unlawfully), or the police bring recording equipment into a cell, any client of mine will say, "*I have been told about your allegations of... I am quite sure that I can satisfy you and deal with all of your concerns, but not today. I shall be saying nothing further, but will be sending in a detailed written statement. Thank you.*"

They then zip it. They do not say "*No comment*" over and over. They say nothing. This simple but effective strategy has become a fantastic part of my business and takes away the fear that people have of an intimidating and frightening interview under caution.

Indeed, in some cases, clients on my advice have merely said, *"I like this cell. I will not go into an interview room. I will stay here. I will not be interviewed."*

Whether in the cell or the interview room, the police soon get fed up and release you. Then, with my help, a detailed, precise statement of exactly what happened is carefully prepared and that is sent in. This replaces the interview under caution, where they fire questions at you, change subjects, try to intimidate you with 'good cop, bad cop' tactics and thrust documents at you to try to catch you out.

This strategy has been hugely popular, especially in sexual, benefit fraud and tax credit fraud cases. A written statement has the same force as a sworn statement. This gets the story across and makes the mitigating points without having to turn up for the terrifying interview which people have seen on TV. It is hugely popular.

I am also completely different. If somebody rings me up, it is usually because they are in trouble or in a potentially life-changing situation. Perhaps their wife is divorcing them, or they have a Court Summons or a letter to attend an interview under caution. Perhaps they have received a non-molestation court order, which prevents them from seeing their children. Whatever it is, my words and advice could literally be life-changing, and I take my job very seriously. The very first thing I ask people, therefore, is, "*Do you have a pen*?" Time and time again, they say no. I say, "*Why are you ringing me up for life-changing advice without a pen? Please go and get one.*"

I did not get my nickname "Rottweiler" by being 'touchy-feely', and this is straightforward advice and hugely important.

HPLC HYLTON-POTTS
LEGAL CONSULTANTS

HPLC LLP
Langthorne Chambers
31 Langthorne Street
London SW6 6JT
United Kingdom

Tel: +44 (0)20 7381 8111
Fax: +44 (0)870 220 0961
Email: law@hylton-potts.com

"Rottweiler" Hylton Potts

When someone is in trouble, they contact a lawyer, but the lawyer is not their friend. '*If you want a friend, get a dog'*, and a lawyer can do more to help you than your friends can.

And I also get clients to laugh to ease the stress. I had one lady client who was so wound up and stressed she could not answer even the basic questions, such as the value of the house or the date of her marriage. She told me that her husband was violent and had hit her several times. She was frightened.

I asked her if she would please give me details of her personal sexual life. She said she was surprised at that question because it did not seem relevant. My answer was, "*It isn't. I just like to hear it*". With this, we both exploded with laughter, and immediately, she began to give me the information I needed. So sometimes the law can be fun!

Pierpoint Morgan, the famous American finance magnate, had his own opinion on lawyers: I think Pierpoint and I would have got on.

"I do not want a lawyer who tells me what I cannot do. I want to hire a lawyer to tell me HOW to do what I want to do."

Another of his famous quotes is: *"Go as far as you can see; when you get there, you'll be able to see further.*" This emphasises the importance of vision, which absolutely applies to the law. I am that type of lawyer.

When you consult a lawyer or a doctor, the one thing you want to know is whether that lawyer or doctor is the best for the job. So why not ask, "*Are you the best lawyer for this job?*" or "*Are you the best surgeon in London for this procedure?*" But nobody ever does.

Staff

Over the years, I have interviewed hundreds of paralegals and solicitors who wanted to work for me. Old and young, white, black and yellow, straight or gay, Christian, Muslim, Sikh or no religion. Glasses, none, clean-shaven, beard, moustache, turban. Blonde, brunette, pretty, plain. You name it, I have seen them all.

In the interviews and their CV, they tell me about their enthusiasm. When I ask them: "*Do you like to meet clients?*" they always reply, "*Yes*," and I say, "*Why?*' and they say, "*Because I like to meet people*" or "*I can get a feel for the case.*" All this is complete nonsense. Meeting clients is mostly just to keep them happy. If one did not actually meet a client, you would probably have more time to do a better job, although nobody ever says that. Instead, the applicant for a job says what they think I want to hear.

The one thing I have never heard in fifty years of interviewing is simply this: "*If you employ me, I will work so hard and make you so much money that you will never want me to leave.*" I would hire in a flash anybody who said that, but all I hear about is how they want to be part of a team, were good at gymkhana at school or excelled in a university debating society, about which I could not give a fig.

I continue to wait but am not holding my breath.

Divorce Wars

"Ah, yes, divorce. See, the problem is that God gives men a brain and a penis and only enough blood to run one at a time." Robin Williams.

Family work, divorce, and child cases provide a fascinating insight into human nature and not all of it is good. The most extraordinary stories emerge. They are often shocking to those who have no idea of the bitterness and anger that can arise during a toxic divorce.

I remember one particularly well. When I lived in Knightsbridge, the house had a large black double bath and every Sunday evening before their bedtime, I jumped in with my two daughters, then aged about 7 and 5, and we splashed around. We made it a 'family tradition' and always a fun end to the weekend before school the next day. Enjoying a splash like that made me acutely aware of the terrible situation of one client.

As chance would have it, this client also had a large double bath and also had two daughters around the same age as mine. He also used to splash around with them regularly and have a bath with them and thought nothing of it, until he got divorced.

There was a battle over money, and the next thing he knew, he was arrested by the police after his wife had alleged improper sexual contact with their daughters.

He did not see them at all for 18 months whilst the investigation ground on and on. He was on bail. Word leaked out, and people tut-tutted, "*There is no smoke without fire*", and even good friends shunned him and had their doubts. He was made so unwelcome he felt compelled to resign from his clubs. At work, there was whispering behind his back or at the coffee machine or water cooler. He was stopped from seeing his daughters, who openly expressed hatred for him, after Mummy 'explained' what had happened, having put words into their mouths.

He did not have any face-to-face contact with his daughters until they were in their early twenties, and then relations were re-established. Then, after the now grown-up children pressed her, the wife confessed to having made the whole thing up to try to get a better divorce settlement.

It is hard to conceive a more wicked thing to do, but this is very typical of the nasty behaviour that goes on in a divorce.

Should It Always Be 50/50?

The law on sharing assets and money is often 50/50, and, as a matter of law, the wife's contribution to running the household and bringing up the children is worth exactly the same as the husband's going out to work (which is a typical situation). With very few exceptions of super earners or entrepreneurs like James Dyson or Richard Branson, the value of bringing up children and going out to work is treated as equal. The needs of (usually) the wife, the main child carer, are given top priority.

Even modern husbands, and especially the older ones, find all this very hard to stomach and get very depressed when they are set back years and have to maybe sell the family house and move into a small flat, giving up all they have worked so hard to achieve.

For example, in one divorce case, my client, the husband, when criticised in Court for being a bully and not treating his wife as an equal, replied indignantly:

"Not true. I even gave her access to my joint bank account."

So, what is the one thing that keeps these husbands sane and even happy? What does not make them despair entirely? It is very simple. They can still 'pull'. A typical divorced ex-wife at 50 will only end up with a divorced man of 55 or more, probably with children and 'baggage'. A typical divorced man of 50, however, can 'pull' a girlfriend, maybe aged 40 or even 35. They often tend to be blonde (profuse apologies to brunette lady readers)!

So this keeps morale up for these men because despite having lost years of their work, life and assets, they can get a boost by having a gorgeous, younger blonde on their arm.

Does that sound shallow? You would do the same.

The Cow

The only winners in divorce or litigation are the lawyers. Have a look at the picture below, which is on my office wall.

The Plaintiff, or husband, is tugging the head. The Defendant, or wife, is tugging the tail. See who is milking it underneath. If you possibly can, keep out of Court. All you are doing is ensuring that your lawyer has a larger Bentley.

Domestic Violence

The common perception is that domestic violence happens on sink estates, and it does. Friday night (payday), and the husband does not come home after work and instead heads for the pub. He arrives back home at about 11 pm, the worse for wear. Earlier that day, the bailiff had called round to take the large plasma TV. The children cried. The wife, at the end of her tether, gets into an argument and pushes him. He pushes her back. She slaps him. He punches her, and she falls, hitting her head. That unglamorous scenario is what often happens on Friday nights.

'NIGELLA COULD WALK AWAY WITH £75M'

We speak to a divorce lawyer about Nigella and Charles' court battle

Leading London divorce lawyer Rodney Hylton-Potts tells **new!**, "The judge won't be interested in who grabbed whose throat. I expect a divorce to be delivered within four months. If they dispute a financial settlement, it'll no doubt become a celebrated case, like with Paul McCartney and Heather Mills. In London, it takes 14 months on average to settle a financial dispute.

Rodney, who isn't representing Nigella or Charles, adds, "A judge would consider their marriage a long one, so the starting point will be 50/50. Everything will go into the pot and be divided by two. With no prenuptial agreement, Nigella could walk away with £75million, but if they do have one it will make a huge difference and severely restrict Nigella's claims. Charles would have no doubt filed for divorce based on her behaviour. It could be as light as, 'She put work before my feelings.'"

But violence is not limited to sink estates. Middle and upper-class marriages are riddled with violence, and invariably, drink and drugs, or both, are involved.

What should a woman (usually) do if she is hurt? She should take photographs of the wound, seek medical attention and make sure the doctor notes the injury carefully. She should put details in a contemporaneous, chronological Word document or spreadsheet on her laptop and tell the police and a lawyer.

I once advised a lady client to buy a light video camera (this was before mobile phones with cameras) to record her husband's violent behaviour. He came in drunk one night and shouted at her. She picked up the camera and pointed it at him, saying, "*I am filming and recording you on my lawyer, Rodney's, advice.*" She recorded the events in a sworn statement later. It read, *"To my surprise, he tore the camera from my hand and smashed it. I now produce a photograph of the broken camera."* It is easy to picture the scene.

To save money, quite rightly, clients often write out an account of how they met their spouses, the marriage, the good times and the breakup. Some of this is priceless.

Example: "*I met my husband when I was working as a stewardess in the first-class cabin of a British Airways long-haul flight. He told me that he was having his Ferrari serviced at Marinello. I fell in love almost at once.*"

One husband told me he was devastated because the marriage was over following his wife's adultery. I asked him if he had ever committed adultery himself. He told me "*No*", which was why it was so particularly painful. I said, "*Before I write anything down, I am going to ask you again. Have you ever committed adultery?*" He paused, then replied, "*Well, yes, obviously abroad.*"

How Much Is A Spouse Worth?

When couples marry, the subject of a pre-nuptial agreement is pretty unromantic. It focuses on a possible breakup, which is horrible. A couple sets forth on the wonderful journey of marriage with high hopes, but the fact remains that one in two marriages fail. How do people know theirs is going to be one of the 50% that succeeds?

The advantage of a prenup is that you can put it in a drawer, bring it out if the marriage ends and just stick to its terms and hopefully stay civil, even amicable. They work, and they should work.

The question often arises, however, of how much a spouse is worth. A typical prenup where one spouse is wealthy and the other has no or few assets protects the assets of the wealthier spouse. Often, a prenup awards to the poorer spouse an amount for each year of the marriage, maybe £20,000 or £50,000, depending on the wealth of the parties.

This is a very tricky subject. The poorer partner discovers what they are considered to be worth by the wealthier partner before they get married.

<u>A Case In Point.</u>

Julia was a New York lady of 45 from a very wealthy Jewish family. Her net worth was something in the region of $10 million. She fell in love with a younger Englishman, Robert, who mended boats, liked animals, had no assets, but was lovely. He had a shock of dark hair and designer stubble and was gentle and good in bed but with no prospects. She wanted a prenup to protect her.

She asked my advice if a yearly amount paid to him was a good plan if the marriage failed. I said that that was an extremely common way of tackling this delicate problem and asked her how much she would like to give him. She pondered and said $500 per year of marriage. After a suitable stunned pause, I told her that would not be upheld by the judge, and she would have to give him a lot more than that. A judge will only approve a prenup if it is reasonable and somewhere approaching fair. She asked me what I thought, and I said a minimum of $20,000 per annum. She was quite grumpy and said that she thought I should be fighting for her. I said that I was, but that was the law.

Eventually, she signed at $20,000 per year and said, "*Please send your invoice, but I am not too happy. I wanted to pay him less.*"

I said, "*Sorry you are not happy but OK, good luck with the wedding. When are you getting married?*" "*In about a month,*" she said. I said, "*Good luck again, but remember that only a month ago, you told me that your husband was only worth, in your view, $500 per year. This included everything that goes with a marriage. Not just the ceremony and sex but companionship, humour, a name, status and the intention to stay together for life (as penguins do!).*"

She considered this and said, "*Do you know, you are right. That is all I really think he is worth.*" She then called off the marriage.

Chalk On The Tyre

In the days when divorce was based on grounds such as adultery (as distinct from 'no fault' these days), private detectives used to obtain evidence of adultery by observing the husband's car being parked outside his mistress's house.

The private detective would put a chalk mark on the tyre, go to bed and come back at 5 am to see if the car had been moved. If the chalk was in the same position, that was evidence accepted by the judges that the man had obviously stayed there overnight.

All over London and elsewhere, there were chalk marks on tyres. Happy days for early morning dog walkers, but confusion from some stealthy husbands who got up in the night to move their car wheel half a revolution.

The Large Breast Fetish

Early on in my career, I was telephoned by a lady, a new client. She said she needed the answer to a legal question. She said that her husband had a large breast fetish and had pressed her to have a breast enlargement operation. She wanted to know whether that was reasonable or cruel and, therefore, grounds for divorce.

Consider now, if you were that lawyer taking the call, how would you have replied?

For what I said, see the end of the chapter.

Beatle Paul And The Linda Tapes

The tabloids are really only interested in about a dozen people in the world. I could walk down Oxford Street naked, snorting cocaine, and the press would not be remotely interested. If, however, Prince Harry sneezes or Paul McCartney goes to the pub, they then go into overdrive. A client of mine discovered he had some tapes recorded by Linda, Paul McCartney's late wife. This is how the tabloids covered it:

Linda to give evidence from beyond the grave in 'dynamite' marriage tapes

Sir Paul McCartney's divorce battle took an astonishing new twist last night after it emerged that his late wife Linda made a series of 'explosive' taped confessions about their relationship.

The 15 audio tapes are said to shed new light on Sir Paul's 29-year marriage to Linda, always regarded as one of the strongest in show business.

Their existence raises the very real possibility of Linda giving evidence from beyond the grave in Sir Paul's messy divorce from their second wife, Heather Mills.

The judge who hears Sir Paul and Lady Heather's case would have the power to order the 20 hours of tapes to be played in Court to establish whether they support Heather's claims that the former Beatle was violent.

Linda poured out her heart to a confidante, with whom she wrote a vegetarian cookery book, before her death in 1998.

Sir Paul's lawyers are so concerned about the contents of the tapes that they contacted the co-author earlier this week demanding that he sign a gagging order, preventing him from making them public.

He agreed to do so, but his legal representative made it clear yesterday that he would give evidence in Court if he were called upon.

One source told the Mail: 'These tapes contain hours and hours of Linda McCartney pouring out her heart in her own words about what was going on in her marriage.

'The material is very private and very emotional. There were times when Linda was in tears. She seemed to find the conversations cathartic.'

Another insider simply described the contents of the tapes as 'explosive'.

A legal representative, Rodney Hylton-Potts, said yesterday: 'The fact that my client has got these tapes tells you a great deal about his relationship with Linda because someone like that would only share these thoughts with a very close friend or confidante.'

The heart-to-heart sessions were mostly recorded in the McCartneys' kitchen in Peasmarsh, East Sussex.

The co-author made frequent visits there in 1988 when he and Linda would discuss ideas for their book Linda McCartney's Home Cooking, published in 1989.

As their friendship grew stronger, Linda began to confide and disclose day-to-day details of her family life.

The tapes were recorded before Linda died of cancer, aged 56.

Earlier this week, Sir Paul's legal team at law firm Sheridans wrote demanding that the co-author give a fresh guarantee to honour the agreement or face legal action. He signed an agreement on Thursday.

But the agreement did not cover discussions he had with Linda, which were not recorded on tape, and he spent yesterday inviting financial offers from newspapers both here and in America for his story.

Mr Hylton-Potts said: 'He is able to talk about conversations which he had with Linda which were not recorded on the tapes.'

Mr Hylton-Potts was struck off as a lawyer in 1997 after being sent to prison for five years for his part in a £2.3m mortgage fraud. He served two and a half years of his sentence before being released on parole and setting himself up as a legal adviser.

Last year, he won the ITV reality show Vote For Me, in which viewers voted for would-be politicians, but was then accused of making racist comments behind the scenes, which he denied.

The existence of the Linda McCartney tapes is an uncanny echo of the devastating videotaped confessions made by Princess Diana during sessions with her voice coach, Peter Settelen, which also emerged after her death.

Like Linda, Diana revealed intimate details of her married life, including the fact that Prince Charles had virtually stopped sleeping with her after the birth of Prince Harry.

In divorce papers leaked to the Daily Mail earlier this month, Lady Heather, 38, accuses 64-year-old Sir Paul of assaulting her on at least four occasions, once slashing her arm with a broken wine glass. She also said he was regularly drunk and took illegal drugs during their four-year marriage.

She is said to be seeking at least £100m of Sir Paul's £825m fortune, but Sir Paul has denied her claims and said he will 'vigorously' defend them in Court.

All ended happily, and the co-author and Beatle Paul met up in Soho. The tapes were destroyed.

Golf And Divorce

St George's Hill Estate in Weybridge, Surrey, has, within its leafy acres, a superb golf course. The 8th hole is the 'signature hole' of some 160 yards from an elevated tee to an elevated green.

Between the tee and the green is a horrible mass of scrub, Heather, sand and general rubbish. George was a fine, experienced golfer with a low handicap. After he married Enid, she took up the game but struggled with children to bring up, never really got into it, but she tried.

They entered a foursome competition. That means that each player hits the ball alternately. So if George hit the first shot, Enid would hit the second, George the third, Enid the fourth and so on. At each hole, the first shot alternated between them.

They came to the eighth hole, and it was Enid's turn to play off the tee. George said, *"Do an air shot."*

Enid replied, *"No."*

George: *"Love you to bits, but you are a beginner. You are not going to get over that rubbish. You are going to duff it, and we will lose the hole. Do an air shot; we add one, and I will then take the second shot."*

"No," said Enid.

Then George said the immortal line, *"I am instructing you to do an air shot."*

Furious, Enid stepped up and did just that, which meant that she made a stroke but deliberately missed the ball. George then stepped up, intending to smash a beautiful shot onto the green, but duffed it completely, and it went about 10 yards. At that point, Enid exploded with laughter, and the other golfers joined in.

George was puce with rage, and that was the end of their marriage. It went downhill from there, with constant recriminations and revisions and featured heavily in the subsequent divorce.

The moral of the tale - do not play golf with your wife!

REPLY TO THE LADY WHOSE HUSBAND HAD A LARGE BREAST FETISH:

"I cannot advise on the telephone. You will have to come and see me."

The Diplomat And The Panties

Abad was from Morocco, where he had a good Government job and a beautiful wife and family. He was suave and diplomatic, although whether he was actually a diplomat became important. His work brought him to London periodically, where he naturally had a mistress who, bizarrely, was also Moroccan. He was also a shoplifter.

On one trip to London, he went shopping in Harvey Nichols, the well-known Knightsbridge store next to Harrods. CCTV evidence showed him moving around the ladies' lingerie section of the store, examining and holding intimate underwear, including panties.

At one point, he could clearly be seen slipping a pair into another shopping bag he had with him, which was from a different store, and he repeated this procedure with other intimate items. Stockings and suspenders, so often a favourite with men, found their way into his stash. He made no attempt to pay.

He was beautifully dressed in a tailored blue suit with a smart overcoat and casually strolled out of the store. He got away by about five yards when four burly security guards stopped him, searched him, found the items and called the police.

I Come On The Scene

It was his arrest that brought him to my door. He brought his mistress with him, who was anxious to help. He said he had no cash and had left his credit card at his hotel, so she used her own credit card to pay my fee.

With that out of the way, and only then, I got to work, and I said I would like to ask him some questions. I asked him who the items were for.

He looked puzzled. I said, *"Were they for your wife? For your friend here, or maybe for yourself?"*.

He looked flustered and blurted out, *"For my wife."*

With that, the mistress shouted, *"Stop the transaction, I will not pay"*. But of course, I refused.

She stormed out, but Abad and I continued working.

He was obviously guilty. He told me about the CCTV he had been shown at the police station when he was being interviewed under caution. Readers may remember that I never allow this because no good can come of it, and people usually talk themselves into a conviction or even a prison term.

It emerged that he was, or at least he said he was, a diplomat. This meant that as a diplomat, Abad would be untouchable and would walk away scot-free. He also said he had mental health problems and was feeling depressed.

I needed no more to trigger me into swinging into action. I invited the Crown Prosecution Service (CPS) to check the online version of the 'Blue Book', which lists the names of all diplomats and told them that I was getting documents from Morocco to prove his status but that they would need to be notarised and translated. If he were a genuine diplomat, he would have immunity from prosecution. He could be told to leave the country but would not get a criminal record.

We referred him to a good private psychiatrist. The doctors that I deal with are not in any way 'bent', nor would you expect them to be, but a good private doctor will certainly write a helpful report if he properly and professionally can, and I know some who will.

We were soon armed with the psychiatrist's report saying that he was depressed and was taking medication, having come off a long flight and was confused when shopping in a foreign country, English not being his first language. The complications of psychiatric reports and a possible claim for diplomatic immunity caused the Crown Prosecution Service to think again and drop the case.

They decided there were far easier targets to go after. This result was only achieved because he had money (or, more precisely, his mistress's money) and could afford to consult me, whereas, on Legal Aid, he would have been convicted and have a criminal record.

This illustrates the two-tier system that exists.

I still remember well the look on his face when I asked him who the purchases were for and his girlfriend's fury after discovering they were not for her. He might have done better if he had said they were for him!

A Prison Survival Guide

These thoughts are mainly for white-collar criminals, but they apply to everybody in a criminal court and at risk of prison.

A criminal trial has three phases: the first phase is the best for the defence when the prosecution presents their evidence. Invariably, witnesses do not 'come up to proof' or do not turn up, and a good defence barrister can probe and show inconsistencies. The end of the prosecution case is often a 'high', with the accused optimistic of an acquittal and going home. The worst fears of the accused have not come to pass. It may be bad, but it could have been a lot worse, is a typical sentiment.

The next stage is the defence stage, when the accused and his witnesses give evidence. That usually ends with a 'low' after cross-examination of the accused by the barrister for the prosecution. Things can often then start to look very bleak. The 'high' at the end of the prosecution case can suddenly look a long way away as the accused looks back on how he performed in the witness box and probably wishes that he could do it again.

The final phase is the tense phase when the judge sums up, and the jury goes out to consider their verdict. When the jury comes back in, you can often hear a pin drop. There is a lot of writing about how long a jury takes to reach a verdict, if that is a good sign, and whether they look at the accused as they come back into Court. Unlike the USA, juries in England and Wales are not allowed to discuss what went on in the jury room, so nobody ever really knows.

If the verdict is guilty and there is an immediate sentence of imprisonment or bail is refused pending sentencing, the first thing to remember is that you are immediately cut off from everything and everyone you know.

Instead of walking out of the dock to join your family, lawyer or friends, you go down a flight of stairs to the dock and then lose all control and all decision-making until you re-emerge, whether it be three months, five or ten years later.

You are then conveyed to a prison in a white prison van called a 'sweatbox'. The cubicles are incredibly claustrophobic. It is like being put into a coffin; it's hot, and panic can set in almost immediately. I suffer from claustrophobia, and when it happened to me, I was in a terrible state. A kind prison officer opened the door and the latch an inch, which helped. As a result of this sweatbox journey, when I arrived at Brixton prison, I was immediately put in the prison hospital. To avoid this, prepare for this issue by being armed with tranquillisers before the last day of the trial and have a doctor's letter to try and get a different mode of transport.

Nobody had told or warned me about this possible experience because criminal defence lawyers' brains and their experience stopped at Court.

Upon arrival at the prison, your property is taken from you. Never take a watch worth more than maybe £10. Do not wear a nice belt or have a fancy smartphone or anything else to mark you out. Just take a couple of paperback books, a Kindle, a small device to play music on, earbuds and any medication you have been prescribed. Anything else, and you will immediately be a marked man. Earplugs are the most important, although you can use small pieces of wet loo paper if they take them away.

Prison officers have a two-way relationship with inmates, and word will get out in a flash if you have a few quid. This is a very bad idea. You need to merge into the crowd and be very boring indeed.

Prisons are full of criminals. This may sound obvious, but a newcomer may think he is in a good crowd of men (or women) working together against oppressive guards. Nothing can be further from the truth. Prisoners, in the main, are scum, merely planning their next crime. They will cheat you (phone cards are the currency), steal from you and lie to you. The prison officers, in the main, are a decent lot and, if treated with respect, will make sure you get the privileges you are entitled to, such as phone calls, exercise and access to the library. Equally, the officers are very badly paid, not very committed and are often bone idle.

In a closed prison, you will be locked up, to begin with, for 23 hours a day. Do not keep a diary or calendar, as this way, time will pass by more quickly.

At some stage in your sentence, you may be allowed to wear your own clothes. Do not do so. Accept the bog-standard prison garb of jeans and a blue and white striped shirt. Whatever you do, do not let a 'Harrods' bag arrive from your family or any hint of wealth, as if you do, you are a marked man.

All phone calls are recorded, so be careful what you say. Never talk or write to anybody out of prison about business because you will then be accused of 'running a business'. I helped a sick friend who had cancer with a will by writing it out for him from prison and posting it to him. This resulted in my being promptly moved from an open prison to a closed one. I did not charge a fee. I was merely helping a friend. I was certainly not running a business, but it made no difference. There was no argument and no appeal. I was sent straight back to Brixton in a sweatbox.

Do not give advice in any shape or form, and do not help with fellow inmates' appeals. Do not become a 'listener' who helps depressed inmates. The 'listeners' are the biggest drug pushers among the inmates, and you will immediately come under suspicion by the prison officers.

The main issue is the fear of the unknown. You will hear dogs barking and gates clanging, and it feels like a German concentration camp; in fact, it is all very professional and orderly, but it really helps to know what to expect.

The worst thing is the noise. The prisoners are completely selfish and will play loud music as long as the lazy prisoner officers let them get away with it, and that is a real problem.

Decide how you are going to use your time. There is no point in feeling sorry for yourself. Make a plan to, for example, get very fit and keep fit. I used to run and exercise six days a week and then really enjoyed my seventh 'rest' day. You could try your hand at writing a book or researching a few things you never had time to do. Consider it a delayed National Service, which I did, and that helped me a lot.

Many prisoners 'find religion' in the hope that this will help them get parole, which usually comes halfway through the sentence. Do not bother; this is a complete waste of time for parole. The only advantage of going to church, apart from religious dedication if that is your thing, is being able to sing and maybe read a lesson to relieve the monotony.

Another useful tip is that putting up 'girly' posters in your cell might discourage homosexual advances.

If there is violence against you, the other prisoners will tell you to "*Sort it out on the wing*". Do no such thing. The Prison Service has an absolute first duty to protect prisoners and, therefore, if somebody punches you, go immediately to the officer and tell them - yes, 'grass them up'. Violence is intolerable, and the staff will help you. "*Sorting it out on the wing*" ends up in a melee of violence and counterviolence and drags you into a gang culture. You would not be violent to your neighbour at home, so why behave that way in prison?

Statistically, if you go into prison married or in a relationship, you will come out divorced or alone. I did. Many men strive to do the right thing by their wives by putting the house and other assets in the wife's name, arranging upfront payments to make life easier, and taking out loans to give her security. Again, I did, and she kept the lot. Be very, very careful.

Most wives do not 'wait' and move on with their lives. Perhaps you would not 'wait' if the boot was on the other foot.

Find somebody, like me, if you like, who has been through the system and has some wisdom and experience and can tell you what to do. I did put everything in my wife's name, feeling great guilt, and was promptly and royally shafted by her when she kept everything and left me, so I came out of prison penniless. So much for '*for richer for poorer, for better for worse*'.

There is a story that when you are released from prison and walk out and away if you look back, you will go back. This is probably an old wives' tale, but take no chances. Eyes front -never look back. My friends recorded my leaving in the following cartoon:

FAREWELL
H-P !!
GOVERNORS OFFICE
REGGIE KRAY
RONNIE KNIGHT
LORD BROCKET
MICHAEL FAGIN
COME BACK!
WE CAN'T MANAGE
WITHOUT YOU.
LEGAL AID IS
NO SUBSTITUTE.
HMP SPRINGHILL
IN THE BOOT
AND BE QUICK
ABOUT IT.
HOPE YOU PACKED
THE VIAGRA!
RHP II
LONDON
JANUARY 1999

Had He Not Been Black

We look at racial discrimination today and jump on any hint of it, sometimes ridiculously accusing people of being racist when all they are trying to say is that our small island is too overcrowded and losing its identity.

I am not saying things are perfect now, but back in the 70's, racism was a real problem.

Chelsea Cloisters is in Draycott Avenue, Chelsea, in a fashionable part of West London near Harrods. It is a large block favoured by business people who stay overnight, often with girls from escort agencies, but also the home to drug dealers or used as bachelor flats.

In the 1970s, a tip-off reached the Chelsea drug squad that a drug dealer was operating on the third floor of the block. They decided to immediately raid the premises with a view to searching the flat, finding the drugs and arresting him.

Plain clothes police officers arrived at the concierge's desk on the ground floor and instructed him very sternly not to 'phone ahead'.

They then entered the lift and pressed the button for the third floor.

Having received some very good cash tips over time from the occupant of the third-floor flat (the alleged drug dealer), the concierge ignored the instructions the police had given him and phoned ahead to warn the dealer that they were on their way up.

Having banged on the door with no reply, the police burst into the third-floor apartment, only to find no sight of the suspect but a window wide open. The suspect had jumped out of the window and fallen three stories down into the car park below.

They rushed downstairs and called an ambulance.

The police report said - and this is a true story and not a joke, I read it - "*Despite being told not to, the concierge telephoned ahead. Upon entering the flat, we found it to be empty, and X had jumped out of the window and landed three floors below, on his head, in the car park. Had he not been black, he would certainly have been killed.*"

And people claim racism abounds today.

A Fisherman's Friend

Whether or not to give evidence and to go into the witness box is a crucially important decision in a criminal trial. If the accused does not go in the witness box, the jury often thinks: "*He must have something to hide. Why did he not go in there and tell us his story?*"

If, however, he does go in the witness box, he is open to cross-examination by a tough Crown Prosecution barrister who could rip him to shreds, so it is always a hugely important decision and one not to make lightly.

I was handling a case of serious aggravated buggery in Reading Crown Court. This carries a long prison term if convicted. The accused and I agonised with Counsel (Tom Shephard) over the lunch break as to whether our client, Nigel, should go in the box at 2 pm to give evidence. The prosecution case was over. The decision was finely balanced. This was Nigel's chance to tell his story to the jury, but would sending him into the box be a mistake?

Nigel said he really could not decide, and we had to go back to Court. The judge said to counsel, "*Mr Shephard, do you wish to call any evidence*?" Still not knowing our client's decision, counsel turned to Nigel, who then nodded. "*I call the Defendant*", said Tom.

The client, Nigel, was a most unattractive character. He had bad teeth and greasy hair and was a bit camp. He made his way to the witness box, and the clerk asked him to state his name and address and to take the oath.

He turned to the judge in a weak, hoarse voice and said, "*I am very sorry, Your Honour, but I have awful laryngitis. I will do my best.*"

This came out as a low, forced wheeze, with the man battling to get his words out. Very impressive and clever, I thought. Odd though. Over lunch, his voice had been fine.

The judge, however, turned to Counsel and said, "*Mr Shephard, I see that your client is having some difficulty with his voice. Would he care to suck a Fisherman's Friend?*"

Quick as a flash, Tom replied, "*I believe, Your Honour, that he would, but he seems to be in enough trouble already.*"

The jury collapsed in laughter, and that is generally a good sign because it is quite hard to send someone to prison when you are laughing. He got off, and miraculously, his voice recovered in time for him to buy the first round.

We Don't Want Your Sort Around Here

Racial discrimination claims can be very profitable for the (usually) black claimant and his lawyer.

In 2005, my black client, Godwin, who was a contractor working in an NHS hospital, having been given permission to use the canteen, went there for his lunch. Godwin was a jolly fellow, a bit fat, and he found his trousers constantly slipped down to reveal a 'builder's crack'.

The canteen was self-service. He placed a hamburger and chips on two separate small plates on the tray and then hid the hamburger from sight by covering it with a napkin.

He went up to the 'white' dinner lady to pay. Eyeing him suspiciously, she shot her hand out, grabbed the napkin and pulled it up, revealing the hidden hamburger. She told him, "*We don't want your sort around here*" - meaning thieves.

We sued for racial discrimination and won £18,000. £18,000 divided nicely by three - I was on one-third.

The Vanessa Sex Letter

Matthew was a typical 20-year-old student living in a hostel. He liked to study history (sometimes), but mainly, he wanted to smoke dope and stay in bed with his rather pretty girlfriend, Vanessa.

One night in the hostel, a fellow occupant, a nutcase, entered Matthew's room with a large knife, spoiling for a fight. It was late in the evening, and Matthew was alone.

They struggled, and Matthew pushed him off and ran, but not before the attacker cut him with the knife, leaving a large slash across Matthew's chest. When healed, this resulted in a huge purple scar which ran diagonally across his chest.

There is a UK government scheme called the Criminal Injuries Compensation Board, which can make large payments to people who are injured, and Matthew asked me to make a claim on his behalf.

The issue of the scar came up, and I asked Matthew how he felt about it. He said he felt pretty cool about it and fancied himself as a potential actor in a James Bond film and that Vanessa thought so, too.

I pointed out gently that some girls might find such a scar off-putting. He got the hint. He must have then spoken to Vanessa.

When I later interviewed Vanessa, she told me that she loved going to bed with Matthew, but since the scar appeared, whenever he took off his shirt, she would be almost physically ill and had difficulty not projectile vomiting across the room.

The Board accepted this and awarded him £27,000 for being less attractive to women and damaging his love life.

The letter Vanessa wrote in support of his claim became known as the 'Vanessa Sex Letter'.

The Peking/Paris Rally & The Angry Ex-Husband

Peter and Jenny were a couple who seemed to have it all. They had a large house in Chelsea in London, a holiday property abroad, two gorgeous children, and two, even more, gorgeous dogs, and Peter was on the Times Richest List. Peter was rugged and handsome, an Alpha male. Jenny had classic English good looks and long, blonde hair.

They had plenty of money to spare, and one of their hobbies was motor racing. They had agreed and intended to go on the famous Peking to Paris Rally in a fabulous restored 2-seater E-type Jaguar sports car.

The Peking to Paris Rally is fashionable and expensive to enter at £59,000 per car. It is now called the Beijing-Paris automobile race and was initially held in 1907 over a distance of 14,994 kilometres. The competitors stop at fashionable hotels along the route. It is all very 'Orient Express'.

Before the next rally dates arrived, however, they separated, and Peter emailed Jenny saying, "*Shame we cannot go on the rally, but that's life*".

Jenny replied, "*What do you mean 'we'?*"

Because she had booked it in her name, she was determined to go to the rally and take her new boyfriend along, which drove Peter into a fury. He became obsessed with it and contacted me.

I was handling his divorce, and he was paying me a lot of money. He told me that he expected me to stop her from going to this rally.

I said, what could I do? He said, "*Just fix it.*" The only thing I could think of was pulling every string I could to get the divorce Court hearing on the day of the rally or so close to it that she could not get to Peking in time.

I did rather well and managed to get the case listed the day before the rally kicked off in Peking. That would mean that she would have to leave Court in Holborn, London, by 2 pm to get to Heathrow to catch the flight to Peking or miss the rally.

Peter was pleased with this, but when we arrived at court at 10 am, that soon changed when we were told that we were first on. Usually, at court, you hang around for hours, often until the afternoon, but that day, other cases had settled out of court, and we were expected by the judge to be in court at 10 am. It looked very likely that the wife would comfortably make the Peking flight.

He took me to one side and hissed, "*I am paying you a fortune. That woman is not to go to the rally. I expect you to do something.*" I threw up my hands in despair, but he meant it. We were called into court.

As we walked from a meeting room towards the court, the alarm bell went off loudly, and an usher came up and boomed, "*Bomb scare, evacuate the building*". Peter turned to me with a huge smile, gave me a high five and said, "*Fantastic. Well done, Rodney.*" I was lucky not to be arrested! Oh, and by the way - it was not me. The ex-wife missed her flight and did not make the rally.

The Murderer And The Leather Jacket

Towards the end of their sentences, prisoners are allowed out for the day. Bicester Village, near the Spring Hill, Oxfordshire Open Prison, where I was at the end of my sentence, was a favourite with the prisoners, as well as with hordes of Japanese tourists. It is a shopping centre with famous brands at much reduced prices and fun cafés.

One of the prisoners, Dave, was a huge man in prison for disposing of a body after a murder. He was part of a debt-collecting team, and the job had gone wrong when they had gone too far and killed the man rather than just roughing him up. Dave got the body into a van and then torched it, but got caught and was serving eight years.

With a few weeks to go before the end of his sentence, he had a day out. He told me he had heard that I was a clever chap, and he wanted my advice, which I readily gave.

He said he was meeting his father, who had £40 for him, and that he, Dave, wanted to get laid. The question was, should he buy a leather jacket or pay for a tart? He was meeting his father at Bicester village, who could arrange either.

I gave it some thought and then said that if he bought the leather jacket, he would not need to go to a tart because if he rocked a cool leather jacket, women would fall for him.

He considered this to be brilliant advice, thanked me warmly, and went off happy.

I was not out that day, but I spent the whole time worried sick, thinking about what would happen if he came back having not 'scored' with his leather jacket. I could picture my broken nose or worse. How stupid I had been to give him advice and stick my neck out.

Fortunately, all went to plan, and he came back with a big smile on his face and the leather jacket, not having had to go to a tart. He said he met a girl in Bicester Village who wanted more than retail therapy.

Never has advice been given so quickly and contemplated so slowly, and never has so many thanks been given to the good Lord for my getting it right!

The Portsmouth Penis Basher

Portsmouth is a naval town, and when the sailors come home from a voyage, they pour off the ships to enjoy all the attractions of the bars and brothels in the vicinity.

Many of them, however, head for the public lavatories, which are so popular that in the men's lavatory, holes the size of a cup have been drilled between the cubicles.

The idea is that the horny sailor places his penis through the hole and receives a welcoming 'hand' on the other side from a like-minded reveller.

My client, however, saw things differently. About 60, balding and with greasy hair, he had been turned down for the Navy and bore a grudge. He took a hammer and waited patiently in one of the cubicles. Before long, a penis found its way through, and the hammer came down.

Just writing this makes my eyes water!

We got him off by asking the over-enthusiastic police if they were being paid there to keep watch. They had pounced shortly after the attack.

It emerged that they had been doing it for free and were not even being paid normal wages, let alone overtime.

The jury, through a mixture of humour and laughter and thinking that the police were pretty unpleasant lurking around without being paid, ignored the judge's strong pressure to convict. They let the man off. The *Portsmouth Penis Basher* remained free to do it again.

What was not recorded is whether the lavatories became less popular in the future!

The Doctor And The Soaps

Lamin Okfore (not his real name) qualified as a doctor in Nigeria. He became a British citizen and wanted to put his skills to good use working in England.

A little-known pre-Brexit loophole existed whereby doctors and dentists did not have to pass the usual doctor's professional examination before qualifying as doctors in the UK. This involved just travelling to Europe for three months to work in any European country, coming back to the UK and then enforcing Europewide E.C. rights. It was all about Freedom of Movement. God help the public. Thank Heaven it has now been stopped by Brexit.

In addition, however, the doctor has to prove that he speaks reasonable English. This new hurdle was introduced as a direct result of one of my African clients, Dr Hussain, who managed to qualify as a doctor despite speaking almost no English. In fact, he was so happy to get qualified that after the hearing at the General Medical Council (GMC) in Manchester, he spoke to the press and said the immortal lines: "*I am so happy to be a doctor. I will have money. Yummy, yummy I can put food in my tummy,"* and the other classics in the cutting below.

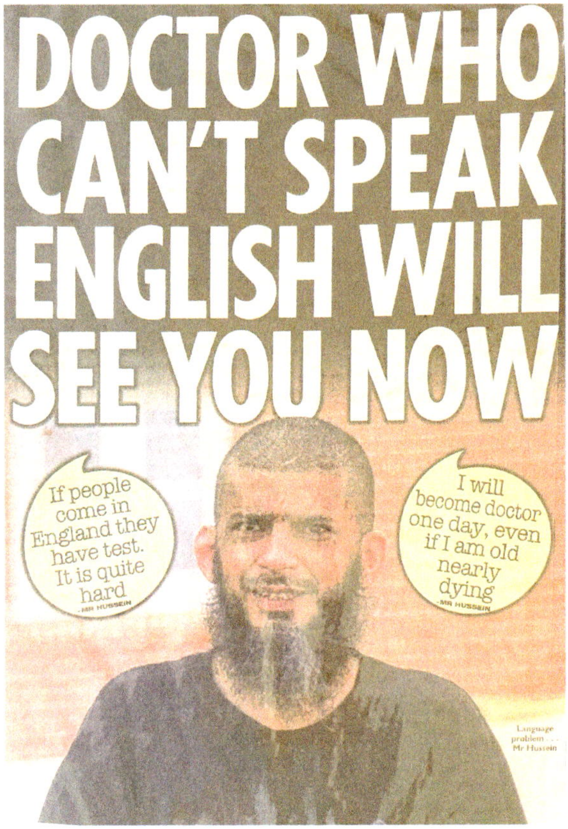

For Dr. Okfore, however, speaking reasonable English was not the problem. His final hurdle was professional experience and competence.

He applied to the GMC for registration but was turned down because there was a gap in his experience in the profession. For about seven months following a car accident, he had not worked, and this became an issue because the GMC are rightly very keen that doctors are up to date with medical practice and procedures. I was instructed on his appeal, and I was representing him at a GMC appeal panel hearing in Manchester when this issue came up.

A GMC panel consists of five doctors or people in healthcare, and they are there to decide appeals from overseas doctors who have been turned down for registration. My doctor client was giving evidence at the hearing, sitting right next to me, when the chairman of the panel said, "*Doctor. Could you please explain how you kept up to date with medical developments and procedures in the seven months after your unfortunate serious car accident?*"

Without missing a beat, he said, "*I watched soaps on TV. I particularly like Chicago Hope and Casualty, but my favourite is Grey's Anatomy.*"

The chairman looked bewildered and said rather sternly to the doctor, "*Are you seriously telling this panel that you kept up to date with medical practice and procedure by watching TV soaps? Is that your case?*"

The doctor switched off his microphone, looked panicky and turned to me, whispering furiously, "*What do I say*?". I said, "*Leave this to me.*"

I had seconds to think. I said, "*Mr Chairman, I believe I can help. In Nigeria, they do not have soaps on TV. Clearly, the doctor thought that these programmes were documentaries, fly-on-the-wall programmes, showing medical practice and procedure.*"

The chairman said he would retire with his colleagues to confer, while the doctor whispered that he was very happy with me and my answer was brilliant.

After ten minutes, the panel came back into the room, and the chairman said to me, "*Thank you, Mr Hylton-Potts. Could you now explain to us how the sex scenes in the soaps fit into your narrative?*" I could feel the heat and embarrassment coming up to my collar and said lamely, "*Sir, I need time to answer that question.*"

I never did answer it, and the doctor was not let loose to operate on you!

The Case Of The Muffled Microphone

Richard liked black women. His black girlfriend was due at his Marylebone flat in central London one Thursday evening in June 2014. The area is now called Fitzrovia, which just means that estate agents can put up prices.

Everything was ready. He had even cooked something decent but, more importantly, had unlimited vintage wines and four lines of cocaine neatly lined up with a credit card to chop it and a pound note to snort it on top of a large biscuit tin.

The music was playing, and he anticipated the evening with some pleasure. His girlfriend was due at 8 pm and was usually punctual. Eight o'clock came and went, as did 8.30 pm and 9.00 pm. He phoned her mobile, only to get a recorded message, and eventually realised he had been stood up.

By this time, he had polished off all the cocaine and half a bottle of wine and was horny as hell, so he set off for the red-light district in his brown Bentley, which was parked in the garage below his flat.

The Adventure In The Brown Bentley

It was raining lightly, and the windscreen wipers went to and fro. He headed for Sussex Gardens, Bayswater, near Paddington station. It is a well-known pick-up place, and there he saw and met a woman. He would never forget the meeting, and what he did or did not say to her would be pored over and scrutinised.

The woman wore a short skirt and had a shock of black hair, rather like Tina Turner. He beckoned her over (that much was undisputed) and lowered the window of his brown Bentley with an electronic button. He then spoke to her, to which she replied, "*You are under arrest.*" She turned out to be an undercover policewoman. He sobered up pretty quickly, but fortunately, the police did not breathe him.

At the police station, he was told that the allegation was that he had said, "*How much to lick my ass and balls?*" and the charge was procuring prostitution, or 'kerb-crawling'. It is an offence for a person in the street to solicit another for the purpose of obtaining paid-for sexual services.

He knew he was in trouble because the words "*Lick my ass and balls*" sounded just like what he liked, so he probably had said it.

Maud At The Police Station

My wife and legal partner, Maud, went to the police station after he contacted me, and she delved into the case. When the police choose a policewoman to play an undercover prostitute, they tend to choose someone who looks the part (Tina Turner hair) and, in particular, has large breasts. This policewoman was no exception. The microphone which they had hidden on her person had slipped between her ample bosoms, muffling the sound.

It was, therefore, very difficult to hear exactly what Richard had said. They played the recording over and over, with the police insisting it sounded like, "*Lick my ass and balls*", while Maud looked suitably puzzled, desperately trying to think of a way out.

In the end, she cried, "*I've got it. What he is saying is, "Do you want to go to Annabel's?"*".

Annabel's was a well-known and fashionable club, and the police knew it. They threw in the towel and let him off. So, no matter how dark things look, never give up and never stop fighting. 'Get Me Off Rod' I may be, but this was a case of '*Maud got me off*'.

The Dentist And The Panties

Mohammed worked hard as a dentist. He was married, had no children, and his life was very much his work. It is widely known that many dentists become exhausted and that there is a high suicide rate within the profession. The exhaustion and the 'downs' are often relieved by the use of drugs and alcohol. Mohammed was no exception.

Most weeknights, after dinner at home with his wife, he used to go online and chat with hookers on porn sites. His wife knew what was going on but just shrugged. She was from Eastern Europe, and part of the unwritten 'deal' that these ladies enter into on marriage is to provide sex on demand, but not demand exclusivity.

Mohammed liked one particular girl he had met online and chatted to, who looked different, fresh and certainly young, which he liked. He sent her various ‘tributes’ such as Amazon vouchers, but the fun started when he messaged her that he would like to have a pair of her used panties.

He paid for these, and they duly arrived (sent to his surgery, private and confidential). He found the experience satisfactory, and his interest in the girl quickened.

He wanted to meet her and eventually did so in a car park in Woking. I would love to tell you it was outside the Pizza Express where Prince Andrew took Beatrice on the fateful night when it is said he did not meet Virginia in 'Tramp' nightclub, but I cannot be sure.

Anyhow, they met in a car park, and Mohammed was very satisfied with the blowjob he received and was very keen to meet the girl again.

They arranged to meet in the car park again, but this time he had booked a hotel room, where they went.

No sooner had they entered the bedroom, and before he could even get his boxer shorts off (and presumably her panties, assuming she had a second pair), the door burst open, and several police stormed in.

It seemed that she was on a list of vulnerable Eastern European girls who were being monitored by the police. She was underage. That became the key issue when he spoke to the police after his arrest.

Most Englishmen know that the legal age for sex is 16, but not everyone knows that the legal age for paid sex - prostitution, is 18. If, therefore, a money transaction takes place with a prostitute and the girl is under 18, the man is in trouble and if she is 13 or less, in really big trouble. It does not matter how old the girl looks if she is 13 or less.

The statutory defence he adopted was that he thought she was 18. These girls dress as what is often called 'jailbait', and they certainly look older than they are.

When he consulted me, he told me that the police had seized his laptop. I asked him whether he had shared information on his laptop about the girl, maybe recommending her to his friends. He said he could not remember because most of the time, he had drunk so much whisky and smoked so much marijuana that he could really not remember what was going on, but he thought it was pretty likely.

All this was important because, as she was a vulnerable teenage girl, he now faced charges of trafficking an underage girl. 'Trafficking' in this case meant driving her from the Woking car park to the hotel and recommending her to his friends via his laptop.

His wife forgave him, but the authorities took a different view. Fortunately for him, he had me. We were able to convince the Crown Prosecution Service that they would not get a conviction because the girl looked 18 and had told him she was 18 (or so he said) and that his wife had forgiven him and would give evidence for him at any trial.

It would not be in the public interest to destroy a man's career when nothing had happened. But this was a close shave.

The moral is - whenever you are on your computer having drunk alcohol and maybe with a spliff in your hand, think twice before you press send!

Short Stories

Courts are intimidating and intended to be. Wigs, gowns, oak panelling, echoing old buildings, work. Speaking in court is nerve-wracking. It takes time for an advocate to get used to it. My first case could not have been simpler. On behalf of a publican, I had to ask the magistrates to extend the pub's normal closing hours from 11 pm until midnight, because there was a wedding on. The pub was called The Old Bull and was in a market town.

All I had to say was a few words.

I rose in court and literally found that my knees were knocking together. I pressed on and managed to get out the words: "*I seek an extension for The Old Bull*". With that, the magistrates and everybody else in the court roared with laughter.

Brush With The Law Society

I was sometimes too outspoken. I once received a very annoying letter from another lawyer, and I replied:

"Dear Sirs, *Fuck off. Stronger letter follows. Yours faithfully."*

I had to grovel a bit to the Law Society, but I still think it has a good ring to it.

Drying Up In Court

A young female barrister I once met had a terrible experience. In one of her first cases, she literally dried up. Nothing came out of her mouth. She was completely tongue-tied and looked more and more embarrassed. An older barrister next to her whispered, "*Drop your papers all over the floor, turn round to pick them up and bend down, keeping your legs straight.*"

This presented an extremely comely bottom to the all-male bench of magistrates, who stared at it very happily. The chairman magistrate said, "*Please take your time and pick up your papers. These things happen. We will wait for you.*"

I often thought of trying it, but as a man in trousers, not a short tight black skirt, I never thought it worth the risk!

Unintended Humour From The Bench

In one case I handled, a lady victim was very distressed giving evidence. It was a late morning session of the day, which ended at 1 pm. She was close to tears. She explained that the accused had placed his hand firmly on her private parts (vagina) and had kept it there, despite her begging him to remove it.

Listening to this, the judge looked at the clock to see that it was almost 1 pm. Thinking of lunch, he said the immortal line, *"Let's leave it there until 2 pm."*

The Penis And Its End

A lady in one case alleged that the accused had exposed himself to her. She could not describe his face, but she could describe his penis so convincingly that it led to criminal charges.

In court, she was asked about the penis and explained that she would know it anywhere again because it "*Had no end*". To make sure that the jury knew what she meant by that, the judge memorably said, "*When you say the penis had no end, do you mean it was endless*?".

Party Coffers

On my travels, I had cause to fly out to the Canary Islands to see a client, Jason Davis, who was under enquiry by the Serious Fraud Office, having been Asil Nadir's stockbroker and caught up in the Polly Peck scandal.

My companion on the trip was a wonderful journalist who told me that in previous years, he had worked at *Hansard*, the body that records parliamentary debates.

He said that he often got the 'graveyard' evening shift when MPs came in after dinner. His job had been to try to decipher what they said, sometimes after they had dined well. His most difficult task was to get down on paper what Ian Paisley, the firebrand Northern Ireland Protestant MP, was saying.

It was the practice to make every effort to write down correctly what an MP said and then send it to him or her for approval before it went into the official *Hansard magazine.* The journalist found himself in real difficulty because he could not understand many of the words from Ian Paisley's remarkable oratory.

A more experienced journalist had suggested that whenever in doubt, he should just insert the words *"murdering Irish bastards"* and send it to the Reverend for approval. This the journalist did and, without fail, it came back ticked and approved every time.

My First Divorce Case

My very first divorce client confided in me straightaway. He explained he was leaving his wife for better sex because he had found a lady whom he found to be much more satisfying.

Although I was young at 25, I knew enough about divorce practice through my training to know that that was a very unusual reason. Most marriages break up because of changing personalities, violence, drink problems or couples just growing apart.

For a man to leave his wife because he got more satisfying sex with another woman is very rare. Such a man would normally find a mistress or go to a prostitute.

He knew this and explained that what he wanted was a lawyer who could appreciate all that. He said: "*You know that look. You have made love to a woman, you are on top of her, and she looks into your eyes, and you look into hers, and you know the look. You know you have really satisfied her.*"

I replied, or rather blurted out, "*I have never seen that look.*" He said: "*Clearly, you were not the right man for that woman, and you are certainly not the right lawyer for me.*" With that, he walked out.

The Chicken And The Neighbour

Sid Caplan was a liquidator extraordinaire. Smooth, with silver hair and beautifully dressed, he was the thinking man's, Arthur Daley. In the 1980s, he single-handedly brought the need for the Insolvency Act 1986 to regulate liquidators because he was operating without being regulated.

He was caught by the Department of Trade and Industry, who set up a sting investigation by wiring up a businessman pretending he had a company that needed to go into liquidation.

Sid told him that there were two sorts of debts. "*There are what we call Crown debts, which are debts owed to the tax man, VAT, etc. We do not pay those. Then there are other debts, such as those owed to you or your friends and family. We do pay those.*"

He was charged with insolvency offences and faced prison. Before the case started at the Manchester Crown Court, he was approached by a journalist from the Daily Telegraph and asked how he felt and whether he thought he would go to prison.

Ever cheerful to the end, he just said: *"Let's just say that last night I took the chicken out of the freezer and gave it to the neighbour."*

All was well, however. He did not go to prison and, in fact, was out of court in record time. He came over to me, I assumed to thank me. Instead, he said, "*That was quick. Any chance of a refund?"*

<u>The 15-Second Pause</u>

Ewan sold personalised number plates on cars, scooters and motorbikes and did very well. The problem was that he sold them more than once, so people ended up with a number that somebody else already owned, which caused great confusion when the first driver was caught speeding in Northumberland, whereas the second driver had no car but only a motorbike in Cornwall.

He was charged and appeared in court. In those days, it was possible to see the judge in chambers before the hearing and say: "*If my client were to plead guilty, what sentence could he expect?"* The judge would then give an indication such as: "*I would not send him to prison immediately, but would give him a suspended prison sentence."*

In this case, I went to see the judge with our barrister JJ Watson, who asked just that. The judge said, *"I would sentence your client to a term of two years' imprisonment but suspend it."* Out we went to see the client to give him the news, and he was hugely relieved and hugged me.

We went into open court. He pleaded guilty. The prosecution outlined the case, and then the judge said: "*Stand up. I have heard from your Counsel. I have read the references. I have taken everything into account and have decided that a prison term is inevitable. I therefore sentence you to two years in prison.*"

The judge then stopped speaking. The client went white. You could see the colour draining from his face. I remember it well because I turned round to look at him, and he was staring at me with a mixture of shock and fury.

After about 15 seconds, the judge went on: "*But I suspend that sentence for 18 months so that if you do not offend again, you will not have to go to prison. Today, you are free to go.*"

Although the client went off to the pub to celebrate, he did not ask me to accompany him. Lesson learned. Always tell the client about the gap between "*I will send you to prison*" and "*but suspend it*".

Judges do it deliberately to frighten defendants and teach them a lesson. This was not a mistake I would make twice.

<u>Bring Him Up</u>

It was late on a Friday in the Oxford Crown Court in 2005. After a long day, the last case was called. A burglar was to be sentenced for breaking into a house near Oxford. The judge said, "*Bring him up*", and the accused was duly brought up to stand in the dock between two burly prison officers.

I was in court as his solicitor, as was his barrister Robert Peters and the prosecution barrister.
Having been found guilty earlier, Robert Peters addressed the judge in mitigation. Then the judge spoke.

The judge said to the accused, "*Stand up. I have heard all that has been said and written on your behalf, including Mr Peter's persuasive words. Nevertheless, an Englishman's home is his castle, and that still means something in this country. You are a burglar, and you broke into a castle. I sentence you to two years' imprisonment. Take him down.*"

The accused turned around angrily and then went down the stairs shouting loudly and audibly, "*You cunt"*. The judge gave no flicker of emotion.

The policemen drifted away, as did the prosecution Counsel, just leaving Robert and I and a prison officer in court. It is never professionally permitted to leave a judge alone in court, so we waited for him to gather his papers and leave. He made no attempt to do so. This was getting irritating. It was after 4.30 pm on a very nice Friday evening in Oxford, and the prospect of a cool pint in a pub next to the river was very tempting.

The judge then said, "*Bring him back up.*" The accused was brought up from the cells and stood between the two prison officers.

The judge said to him, "*After court today, I will be driven in a chauffeur-driven Daimler accompanied by my Marshall. I will be driven to my house on the Thames. When I get there, my French wife* (emphasis on French*) will be waiting for me, with a delicious dinner in the garden and some cold white wine."*

"You, however, will not be going to the river. You will be going somewhere else. You will be going to Oxford prison, where people will spit in your food, and you will make new friends."

The judge paused and then looked hard and directly at the accused, *"Now who's the cunt. Take him down!"*

The Judge And The Springs

I once met a judge at Henley Regatta, before whom I had a case which was part way through. I jokingly asked him what would happen if I put a case of champagne in the boot of his car. He looked at me sternly and said, *"You should be very careful. The springs are very weak."*

Mr Whyte And PC Black

I do not tell jokes. When I tell the following story, people often say what a good joke-teller I am, but I can assure you it is absolutely accurate word-for-word.

A Mr Whyte, spelt with a 'y', drove a white van. He was a general builder operating in the Putney/Wimbledon/Richmond area in southwest London. It was a hot Wednesday afternoon on the 30th of May 2007, and he had had a hard, long day.

He took a chance at some traffic lights and made a right turn where he should have gone straight ahead. He was seen by a police car driven by a black officer who was called, yes, he really was – PC Black!

The police car drove up behind the white van with its siren on and signalled for it to stop, which it did. PC Black jumped out. PC Black came up to Mr Whyte and pointed out to him that he had turned right against a road sign, which was an offence.

If Mr Whyte had just said sorry, he probably would have got away with a short telling off or a caution, but he was in no mood for that. He was hot, tired, late and irritated and could see no harm had been done. He therefore told PC Black what he thought of him and finished by saying, *"Fuck off. At least I am British. I was born here. I don't have to take this from you."*

PC Black arrested him and placed him (with help from other officers) in handcuffs, not for the motoring offence but for aggravated racial harassment. He said later that Mr Whyte must have been referring to the colour of his skin and took him to be a foreigner.

Upon arriving at the police station, Mr Whyte had his photograph and fingerprints taken and was then questioned. In an extremely unusual move, however, the police were so short-staffed that PC

Black had to interview Mr Whyte himself. This would normally be done by an entirely separate officer for good practice reasons.

After running through the facts, PC Black asked Mr Whyte, *"When you said, 'At least I am British', what did you mean?"*

Mr Whyte said, *"I meant at least I was born in Britain, unlike you."*

PC Black explained that he was as British as Mr Whyte and took offence at the language.

The interview is an absolute classic. I used to use it at clients' lunch parties for role play, but at one very drunken lunch, all the copies got lost.
Anyhow, the lesson is (as Mr Whyte said at the end of the interview), *"I think I have said enough"*.

<u>JJ Watson</u>

JJ Watson was a brilliant barrister whom I briefed regularly for many years up until his death in the early 2000s. He was a former Royal Navy pilot and had been captured in Indonesia. He was once shot down and parachuted into the jungle, but the wind carried him to one of the main streets in Jakarta. He was the only pilot on record to be arrested by a traffic policeman on duty.

He was tortured. He was spreadeagled, and a sharp bamboo pole shoved up his rectum. The stern advice is only to give 'name, rank and number'. I give nothing away by saying that JJ told me that the reality is rather different. "*I would have given them my grandmother's inside leg measurement."*

JJ was a caricature of himself. Dark hair, sideburns, double-breasted striped charcoal suit with waistcoat and a gold watch chain. He had the florid face of a drinker, which he was, and he chain-smoked.

He was in court one day when a young lady barrister doing her first case became very flustered and fainted in court due to a heavy period. JJ was at his best. He escorted her to the ladies' robing room. He then returned to court and spoke to the judge. He explained that she was indisposed and asked that the case "*be adjourned until the 'morrow'*". I have no idea why barristers and judges talk such nonsense. But they insist on saying "*the morrow*" not "*tomorrow"*. They insist on saying*, "The court will consider what you have had to say*," rather than "*I* (the judge) *will consider what you have to say*". All old fashioned, baffling nonsense. The last time I looked, a court was a building, not a person.

Anyhow, the judge was sympathetic and adjourned the case until the 'morrow'.

The lady barrister emerged from the ladies robing room and was effusive in her praise for JJ. She said, "*You have been absolutely wonderful. The least I can do is offer you a lift back to London.*" JJ accepted.

As they were driving past the lady barrister's flat in Hammersmith, she said, "*JJ. You have been so wonderful. I really would like to thank you. Would you like to come up to my flat for a drink or something?"* She said '*something*' suggestively. Her meaning was clear.

Without missing a beat, JJ replied the immortal line, "*That is the most kind, my dear, but bearing in mind the time of the month, I do not think I will bother."*

<u>Who Owns Your Sperm?</u>

Possession is ten-tenths of the law.

When Boris Becker dropped by a London restaurant in 1999, he had no idea his bill would be so enormous: £2 million. That is the amount he paid to settle a paternity claim brought by a waitress who claimed she had a single sexual encounter with him that night.

Becker insisted he only had oral sex, and his lawyers suggested the waitress, a sometime model, had inseminated herself. Legally, the how, where and why of the child's conception are irrelevant. British courts have ruled that regardless of the circumstances behind a man's becoming a father, he has to support the child.

After insemination, a man has no similar protection of his right to decide whether to become a father. But at what moment does he lose that right? Is ejaculation the legal point of no return? Does the fact that a woman lies to him about her birth control, retrieves his semen from a discarded condom, sexually assaults him after he has fallen unconscious or rapes him before he has reached adulthood mitigate in any way his financial responsibility?

The answer, absurdly, is no. At present, no matter how a woman gets her hands on his semen (short of using a sperm bank, where the donors are anonymous), a man has no chance of avoiding the financial obligations of unexpected progeny. It is an inequity in the legal system that allows women not only to 'steal' semen but also to demand money from unwilling fathers - a way of finding a sperm donor who also pays for the child.

Lying to a man about using birth control is the most common situation where men get roped into fatherhood. Consider the recent case of the British telecom executive. He met a woman at a nightclub, had a fling and expected the relationship to end when she left for an extended trip to Australia. Instead, she called to say she was pregnant with his child.

Having used protection throughout the relationship, the executive felt he had been a victim of bad luck. But the woman admitted, first during an emotional phone conversation and later in a confessional letter, that she had taken his semen from a discarded condom while he was in the shower. Despite this, a court ordered the new father to pay support. He now finds himself on the hook for £167,000 until the child turns 18.

Until there is a law against misappropriating sperm, men who take reasonable precautions not to inseminate or who trust their partners to be honest about birth control have no recourse should a pregnancy occur. Because, as any number of men can attest, semen can be the gift that keeps on taking.

Sling Your Hook

Tom (not his real name) was a big Chelsea football fan who never missed a home game and also managed to attend most away games. Up the Blues! His real interest, however, was not the skill of the players on the pitch but trouble. He loved having a set-to with the opposing team's fans. He called it harmless banter, but sometimes it took a more sinister turn. He was 28, worked out in the gym most days and was a karate black belt.

On 13th February 2010, Tom went to see Chelsea play at Stamford Bridge, their home ground, in west London. The opposing team was Cardiff and there was fierce rivalry. Historically, there had been trouble when the two teams clashed. It was the FA Cup fifth round and a big match. The teams had not met for 18 years. That day produced some of the worst football violence since the 1990s. A total of 96 people were convicted, many of serious offences, with long jail sentences and long bans from attending football grounds handed out.

The two teams' supporters had form. When a Chelsea fan was killed at Huddersfield, the Cardiff fans sang the Welsh national anthem. The responses were chants about Aberfan, the site of a landslide which wiped out an entire primary school in the Welsh valleys in the Sixties.

During the 2010 game which Tom attended, two huge inflatable sheep were flown above the Cardiff fan's stands whilst the Chelsea fans chanted about doing something unmentionable to sheep.

Trouble was in the air after the game. Police sirens were wailing. The local hooligans were called the 'Chelsea Headhunters' and were out in force dishing out their own savage brand of football violence on rival fans at football grounds around the country. Many had been jailed in the 70s and 80s, but they got together on that fateful day for one last reunion. Many were middle-aged and potbellied but had come out of retirement for one last dust-up. This was a chance to rekindle the tribal camaraderie and blood-filled adrenaline that they missed.

One of their trademark injuries was the infamous 'Chelsea Smile', so called because the victim's face was sliced from the edge of the mouth to each ear. Ronnie and Reggie Kray would have been proud.

Cardiff had its own gang of hooligans called the ‘Sole Crew’, who were up for a fight with the Chelsea hardcore group. Suspecting trouble, the police insisted on a noon kick-off to keep the drinking down to a minimum, but signs of trouble came in the morning. There were stories of up to seven pints being drunk and lines of cocaine being openly snorted in pubs before the game.

One policeman lost an eye. Another had his jaw broken and lost four teeth after being hit in the face with a rock. A pregnant woman told the court later how she was forced to speed away in her car on the King's Road, near Chelsea's Stamford Bridge ground because she feared for her life and that of her unborn child.

Tom's Day And His Defence

At the end of the game, the crowd poured out, and many, including Tom, made for the 'Butcher's Hook', a pub opposite the ground. After attending the exciting match alone, Tom was walking along minding his own business, looking forward to a pint, when he was hit on the back of the leg by a rock. In fear and fury, without thinking, he picked it up and threw it back in the direction from which it had come. The rock sailed over a mounted policeman and landed harmlessly. That was fortunate for Tom because it could have landed anywhere and done real damage.

The rock he threw was pretty big. It can be seen below, captured on CCTV.

Anyhow, who could blame someone for reacting when hit by a big, sharp rock on the leg? And that, Your Honour, is the case for the defence.

The Prosecution Version.

The prosecution took a different view. The police hunted Tom down weeks later, using CCTV footage, having been through thousands of images and using facial recognition technology, which was then in its infancy. The prosecution barrister from the Crown Prosecution Service (CPS) told the jury that it did not matter whether Tom had been hit on the leg or not, although CCTV had not picked that up. What mattered was that he had hurled a missile over a mounted policeman's head and could have done real damage or serious injury. The incident was partly caught on CCTV, which the jury watched enraptured. The white rock is clearly visible.

Preparations For The Trial

Tom had no previous convictions and came from a supportive family who attended court. His father was particularly close to him and sat in on all the meetings with me.

For the trial, I rehearsed with Tom the evidence he would give. Coaching by lawyers is not permitted, but it is perfectly permissible, and indeed desirable, to explain to a client what questions to expect and what the awkward points could be. I met him in my kitchen, where we could spread out the photos on the table. He told me about his karate skills. For fun, I asked him for a demonstration. He got up, whizzed around and gave a backward, high karate kick, precisely striking a legal lever arch file on my kitchen table. This man was a walking, fighting machine.

After a long and expensive trial, the jury could not agree and was discharged, and a second trial was arranged.

This became expensive for Tom's father, who was paying me, and so to help out, I suggested that I meet Tom again, free of charge, to prepare for the second grilling in cross-examination. A re-trial is similar to the first trial but never quite the same. Both sides have hopefully learned from their mistakes and their strategy decisions, good and bad.

The message came back that Tom did not want to meet me for another run-through. He was completely confident he could handle the judge and jury at the second trial. So be it. He was convicted and sent to prison.

I told him at my last meeting with him and his father that if he went to prison, he should say that he was in for VAT fraud. That way, people would leave him alone. That held no interest for him. He let it be known that he was in for football violence and fighting and that he could "*take care of himself*". His father stressed to me that he had been brought up to stand his ground and fight. He would need to.

The last I heard, he had had a thoroughly good kicking.

So when you sling your hook at the Butcher's Hook or get into trouble, listen to your lawyer and do not be a smart arse.

13. 02. 2010 14:15

He Likes Big Horses

When a person in England or Wales makes an offer on a property and exchanges contracts, a 10% deposit is payable. If the buyer cannot complete, perhaps because he could not get a mortgage, he forfeits the 10% and the seller keeps it. This is widely known. What is not widely known is that it is not always the end of the story. If the property has gone down in value for other reasons, such as a downturn in the economy or an announcement of a planned route for a new motorway, the seller can claim more than just the 10% from the buyer.

This is the problem that confronted Peter. Peter was an early retiree in his late 50s. He had had a long and distinguished career in administration in the NHS. Anyone doing that deserves a medal!

It was 2008, and he and Jane, his wife, had set their hearts on a large house near Newbury in Berkshire, which was on the market for £3,000,000. It was not a mansion, but it was a large six-bedroom house with four acres of land and stables for twelve horses. The house was near a railway station for travel into London, and they loved its charm. It was straight out of a Jilly Cooper novel. They expected to see Rupert Campbell-Black riding up the drive any minute.

Above all, they could picture themselves giving dinner parties and playing hide and seek with their grandchildren.

They went ahead with the purchase, having been assured by their mortgage broker that getting a mortgage would be no problem because of John's substantial pension and the fact that Jane, although earning much less, was much younger. They exchanged contracts and paid the 10%, namely £300,000. Completion was set for two months, which was fine because their broker had told them it would take no more than six weeks maximum to get the mortgage. Time flew. Six weeks is not a long time, and so it proved. Two months later, there was still no offer. Peter and Jane were becoming very worried indeed.

The Banking Crisis

Things then got worse. The economy took a dive. There was a banking crisis, and property prices went into freefall. There was to be no mortgage offer. At one point during this period, the banks stopped lending completely.

Peter and Jane were bitterly disappointed. They had not only missed getting the house of their dreams, but they would have to forfeit (lose) the £300,000 deposit they had paid, which was a large chunk of their savings and retirement pot. Nevertheless, they put it down to experience and started looking for something much cheaper to buy, but then things took a real turn for the worse.

They received a legal letter saying that because the house had reduced in value by more than £1,000,000 (it had gone down from about £3 million to £2 million), the owners wanted the balance. In other words, the owners wanted the £1 million that they had lost by not selling to Peter and Jane. They gave credit for the £300,000 deposit, which they had already received and kept, but they wanted another £700,000 plus interest plus their legal fees.

This would have ruined Peter and Jane. Their solicitor told them that they could do nothing except hope that the house would sell and the market would improve, but there was no sign of that. Their only hope was that somebody would make a decent bid for the house, which would convince the owner that the house would sell and he should wait to get a better price rather than go to court and possibly bankrupt Peter and Jane. Unfortunately, there were no new buyers on the horizon.

We Come To The Rescue

At this point, Peter and Jane consulted me. I always try to tell it how it is. Often, the solution is staring you in the face, and this was such a case. As so often in my legal life, Maud, my wife and legal partner, came up with the solution.

About two weeks later, a glamorous, blonde bombshell in a chauffeured black Bentley arrived at the house by appointment with the estate agent. She was beautifully dressed, haughty and entitled. She exuded wealth and confidence.

She went around the house commenting on what she did and did not like, and she was not always polite. She was quite scathing about some of the taste of the furniture in the house. Entering the kitchen, she said, "*I expect it is the sort of place that has fish knives.*" Having fish knives can be social death. She said that various things would have to go, but on the other hand, the stables would be ideal because her husband liked riding.

The estate agent (who, as a breed, often tend to be rather dim public school boys, who wear jackets without sleeves for some reason, with corduroy trousers and carry clipboards) asked her what sort of horses her husband liked. At this, she slightly lost her composure, having no idea at all about horses and blurted: *"He likes big horses."* The correct answer would, of course, have been old horses. She later said that she thought she got away with it.

She told the estate agent that she loved the house, and indeed, the next day, she made an offer of £2.7 million. The owner considered this. He must have noted that this new offer was closer to his initial £3 million sale price than to the current supposed reduced value of £2 million. He realised he should reconsider going to court with an uncertain outcome and maybe wait to see if this offer produced an exchange and completion - that is, the offer from the haughty blonde. That would be better than going to court against Peter and Jane.

Mediation

At this point, we suggested mediation. Mediation is usually a complete waste of time, where people shuttle to and fro between two rooms, not talking to each other, while some retired judge or other worthy in the middle tries to get everybody to settle. A mediator is not remotely interested in fairness or getting the right deal for the situation. His only concern is to get a settlement, any settlement, good, bad or indifferent. He can then trumpet on his website that he has a high percentage of successful mediations.

Despite this, it suited our tactics (delay) to have a mediation, and this was set up. Maud and I were due to go with Peter and Jane, and the seller was going with their lawyer and, of course, the mediator. We were already there in a room, waiting to go into the joint mediation meeting, when our opponent, the seller, said that they would like the estate agent to attend as well and that he was on his way. Maud had to get out of there fast. She had been the haughty blonde who viewed the house and made the offer - and now here she was on the Hylton-Potts legal team. I will not pretend that she went out crawling on her hands and knees under a window, but it was close. Anyway, the estate agent did not spot her, and she got out of there fast, and the mediation went ahead.

Things were not going well, and it looked as though they were going to take Peter and Jane to court despite conceding that there were offers in the wind. We said the seller should wait for a better offer rather than risk a long and expensive court case, which fell on deaf ears, and it was clear they were going to go to court. I then changed tactics.

Having gone to take an imaginary phone call, I returned and asked to see the other lawyer privately. I made a show of looking thoroughly fed up and angry.

I explained that the promised payment from the client by cheque for my fees had not been met and that his cheque had bounced. I said: *"He has not got a pot to piss in, and I am afraid I am off. He has not paid me, and I would not waste my time going anywhere further. He is a total waste of space. You will never collect on any judgment."*

Off I went, apologising for not staying to continue the mediation. I told them I was not going to stay and would not work for free. Astonishingly, they took my word for it. They never made any attempt to check Peter and Jane's wealth. They never asked questions, nor did they request an affidavit of financial standing or bank statements. They never put in an expert, private detective or accountant to make enquiries. They just took my word for it. They never bothered Peter and Jane again. So we had very satisfied clients, but we always remember the close shave of *"What sort of horses does he like?"*

We never discovered what happened to the house, but maybe one day, it will feature in a Jilly Cooper film.

Fighting For Fathers

One of the saddest aspects of my legal work is helping fathers have contact with their children where the mother is implacably opposed to it or certainly wants to restrict contact as much as possible. It is also the most rewarding for me when a father wins.

You may remember Robin and Batman on the window ledge of the Royal Courts of Justice.

We smile at these images, but behind them, there are tragic and desperately sad tales.

Sometimes, a mother has good reason, such as a father who has perhaps taken drugs or been drunk with the children, but very often, it is merely a tactic to get more money.

All the law books and judges say that money and children should never mix. Do not believe a word of it. It happens every day. A father might travel for hours in busy Friday afternoon traffic to pick up the children, only to be told on the doorstep that they have '*developed a cold*' at the last minute and because a mobile phone was not charged, he could not be notified. In effect, the mother can bugger the father around hugely and very frequently does just that.

One of the weapons mothers use is to move away. Great attention is paid to child abduction, where one parent (usually the mother) takes, or threatens to take, the child abroad, especially if they are not originally from the UK. What is less known is the tactic of moving within the UK.

If the mother (who is usually, but not always, the main carer of the children) wants to hurt the father or press him for more money, she can move as far away as possible within the UK, e.g. Cornwall or Northumberland, and then pretty well destroy his attempts to have regular, perhaps fortnightly contact, because of the expense and time involved in travel. A judge can stop this.

Social Workers And CAFCAS

During the court process, the father will meet a social worker, usually via a Court entity called The Children and Family Court Advisory and Support Service (CAFCAS), probably for the first time in his life. On my website, I have a rather amusing video which you might want to click on. Go to the home page and click on https://hyltonpotts.com/l/fighting-for-fathers

In essence, I prepare the father for what the social worker will be like. What I said in the video came up during one of my cases:

The barrister for the mother (I was advising the father) complained to the judge that on my website, I described a social worker as likely to be *"a fat lesbian, wearing green tights, who votes SDP Liberal and eats muesli for breakfast in a scrubbed pine kitchen."*

The judge had to immediately raise the blue notebook he was writing in to cover his mouth, but I could tell from his eyes that he was finding it incredibly difficult to contain his mirth.

Perhaps I was a bit harsh, but you get the general idea.

I had one father who had a conversation at his home with a social worker. The social worker (a lady, although I have no idea whether she was fat or lesbian) said, *"If I recommend to the judge that you see your children just once as a trial experiment, what would you say to them?"*

The father replied, tearfully but without any hesitation, *"I would tell them that I love them so much and miss them."*

The social worker said, *"Oh no. You cannot say that. That would put them under far too much pressure."*

The father replied, *"Get the fuck out of my house."*

After that, the father did not see his children for 18 months. It is essential to 'play the game', take expert advice, and watch out for green tights.

I fight for mothers too, but there should be no 'winners and losers' amongst the parents. The only winners should be the children.

Refusing A Blow Job

Would a man ever refuse the offer of a blow job from his amorous wife? That was the issue in a case I handled.

Richard and Peggy seemed to have it all. A beautiful house and rental properties, race horses and a collection of classic cars, including a red open-top Jaguar E-Type. They had a luxurious lifestyle and enjoyed multiple cruises every year.

Their problems started with the fact that wherever they went (as so often appears in the stories in this book), heavy drinking played a large part in their lives.

One evening in 2013, they drove to their local pub for supper, but food played little part. Afterwards, neither of them were even sure that they had had anything to eat. They certainly had lots of pre-dinner drinks and probably drinks instead of dinner, and certainly drinks after dinner, if dinner had been ordered at all. Having driven to the pub, Richard most unwisely decided to drive back.

The pub was quite near their house, and they lived in the country. They did what many drivers do, which is to take a chance on a cold winter's night. The thought of having to get up the next day to go and collect a car (probably with raging hangovers) was not an attractive one. Peggy had been very amorous during the boozy pub session, kissing and nibbling Richard's ear and making suggestive noises, which he found very agreeable.

Upon entering the car, Richard sat behind the driving wheel and Peggy became even more amorous. She decided to give him a blow job. She turned towards him, but he just wanted to get home safely. She would not take no for an answer, however, and began to unzip his fly. He tried to stop her, but she was determined. He forcefully pushed her away, and they had a blazing row. They drove home in silence.

When they got home, they had more drinks and were still arguing until Richard fell asleep on the sofa. All would have been well had she just gone to bed and let the situation diffuse, but she was so angry that she hit him over the head using an old-fashioned three-bar electric heater. This woke him up. In a blind and drunken fury, he beat her up very badly, breaking her finger and bruising her ribs. She called the police and he was arrested.

He was charged with actual bodily harm and went to prison, serving two years.

While he was in prison (as so often happens), Peggy moved swiftly to divorce him and clean out all the assets. She emptied the joint bank accounts, sold the car collection and diverted all the rental income her way while he floundered in prison.

In a divorce, the starting point for all financial splits is 50/50. Conduct is very rarely taken into account by the judge, however bad. Some judges feel pressure to give one party more than 50% if there has been paedophilia or very serious violence. Still, generally speaking, they will only do so when the injuries (not always to the wife) are so severe that they are long-term, for example, injuries stopping her from earning her living.

In this case, Peggy's lawyers argued that she could not face any new future relationship with any man, because she was badly traumatised and had post-traumatic stress disorder ('PTSD').

I was advising Richard. Upon going through her bank statements, we discovered that within weeks after the attack, Peggy had joined a dating site and had made several monthly membership payments. This did not align with her claim that she could not have a relationship with any man.

That information, in itself, would not be sufficient because no doubt Peggy would argue that she tried a few dates, but the outcome was not successful. She could not take things any further due to the trauma she had suffered. What we needed was a detailed account from a real person who could give sworn evidence in court that she was capable of a normal relationship and, better still, including sexual relations.

The idea formed in my mind to instruct an enquiry agent of the right age and interests, in accordance with the wife's required profile, to make a match. We just needed a volunteer.

So the question for the reader is whether you (if you are, or were, a man) would take up this task of being the private detective and meeting her and whether, if you were that man's wife, you would object.

And, of course, do you think any man would refuse a blow job? Answers on a postcard, please.

Flo From Blow

Edward and Sophie (no, not the Duke and Duchess of Edinburgh) liked to drink. In fact, they liked to drink so much that when they got divorced, the judge was so worried about the safety of their only son, Francis, aged 8, that he ordered them not to drink alcohol during the periods either of them was looking after the boy, and also not to drink 24 hours before he came to stay.

Edward had feared not seeing his son at all and, therefore, after I successfully obtained a Court Order that he could see Francis 50% of the time, he was so happy with the result that he decided to celebrate. Forgetting the restrictions about alcohol, he got absolutely smashed on a Saturday night and fell over flat on his face on the pavement outside his house in Mayfair, badly bruising and grazing his nose and cheek.

He woke up the following day (Sunday), which was only 24 hours before he had to collect his son under the watchful and suspicious gaze of Sophie. She would be more than ready to pounce if she had any hint that he had been drinking in the previous 24 hours. By 'pounce', I mean that she would have notified her lawyers, possibly having taken a photograph of his face and demanded a blood alcohol test by court order within 24 hours. Edward and his 50% contact would be doomed.

Apart from the seriousness of contempt of court, which can lead to short prison sentences, his time with the child would definitely be reduced or even stopped altogether, or he might have to suffer the indignity of only seeing his son at a Contact Centre, supervised by social workers. This solution is mainly used for violent men, ex-prisoners and so on, but is more widely used than is realised.

He contacted me early that Sunday morning for advice. What advice would you give? Most lawyers would be thinking 'legally' of a postponement or some sort of variation or court action, but, as on so many occasions, my brilliant wife and business partner, Maud, and her lateral thinking came to the fore.

An hour later, the doorbell at Edward's Mayfair home rang and he answered. "*I am Flo from Blow*," said the camp makeup artist Maud had arranged.

He carefully made up Edward, expertly covering up the bruises, so that on the handover the following day, when Sophie dropped off their son at his father's house, she did not notice a thing.

All went well until the end of the contact period, when the boy, upon returning to his mother, was asked how things had gone with Daddy. He said he had had a lovely time but then said: "*Mummy, why does Daddy wear makeup*?"

In Closing

I hope you have enjoyed reading this book as much as I enjoyed writing it. Along the way, what did I realise?

A crumpled £50 note is still worth £50. So, whatever happens to you, and however "screwed" or "screwed up" you feel, remember, you still have value.

Now, some Rules for Life.

Never stand between a dog and a lamppost.

Artificial intelligence is no match for natural stupidity.

Experience is a wonderful thing. It enables you to recognise a mistake when you make it again.

Nobody cares if you cannot dance well. Just get up and dance.

A person who is nice to you but rude to a waiter is not a nice person.

Never be afraid to try something new. A lone amateur, Noah, built the Ark. A large group of experts built the Titanic.

And one that got me into all sorts of trouble. Never go to bed on the same day you get up on.

And finally, never, never give in, and never, never give up.

Thank you for joining me through these stories. I hope you have laughed, especially at my expense, because I laugh at life every day.

I still run a busy legal practice with fascinating new cases every week. Watch this space for the next book.

Thank you.

Rodney Hylton-Potts

About The Author

Rodney Hylton-Potts qualified as a solicitor in 1970 and was hugely successful. He handled fascinating and often high-profile cases from his Knightsbridge offices.

In 1996, disaster struck, and he served a prison term following a conviction for mortgage fraud.

On his release, he did something unique, which was to advise in direct competition with qualified solicitors. This became a great success, bringing him a large variety of fascinating and often humorous cases.

Relying upon his lifetime in the law, he is able to lift the lid on real law and provide a fascinating and often amusing insight into what actually goes on in the legal world.

Appendices

Page 303 Chapter 3 - R v Tan

Page 315 Chapter 7 - Nothing Like A Dame

Page 322 Chapter 9 - R v Fraser Marr

R v Tan and others

COURT OF APPEAL, CRIMINAL DIVISION

MAY LJ, PARKER AND STAUGHTON JJ

Hearing dates: 7, 8 DECEMBER 1982, 10 FEBRUARY 1983

Criminal law - Disorderly house - House used by one prostitute for provision of sexual services - Prostitute advertising that such services available there - Prostitute seeing only one client at a time - No one else present when prostitute providing services for client - Whether prostitute keeping a 'disorderly house'.

Criminal law - Prostitution - Living on earnings of prostitution - Man living on earnings of prostitution - Offence for a 'man' to live on earnings of prostitution - Accused a male at birth but subsequently undergoing sex change operation - Accused living on earnings of prostitution - Whether accused a 'man' living on earnings of prostitution - Sexual Offences Act 1956, s 30.

Criminal law - Prostitution - Living on earnings of prostitution - Male prostitution - Prostitute a male at birth but subsequently undergoing sex change operation and working as female prostitute - Accused living on prostitute's earnings - Whether accused living on earnings of prostitution of 'another man' - Sexual Offences Act 1967, s 5(1). 12

A single prostitute who provides services in private premises to one client at a time without spectators is guilty of the common law offence of keeping a disorderly house if it is proved that the services provided are open to the public and are of such a character and are conducted in such a manner (whether by advertisement or otherwise) that their provision amounts to an outrage of public decency or is otherwise calculated to injure the public interest to such an extent as to call for condemnation and punishment (see p 18 g h, post).

R v Higginson (1762) 2 Burr 1232, R v Rogier (1823) 2 Dow & Ry KB 431, R v Berg, Britt, Carr é and Lummies (1927) 20 Cr App R 38, Shaw v DPP [1961] 2 All ER 446, R v Quinn [1961] 3 All ER 88 and R v Brady [1964] 3 All ER 616 considered.

A person who was born a male and remains biologically a male but who has undergone a sex change operation is neverthelesss capable of being convicted under s 30a of the Sexual Offences Act 1956 of being 'a man' who lives on the earnings of prostitution. Similarly, if such a person engages in prostitution, a man or woman who lives on that person's earnings as a prostitute is guilty of the offence of living on the earnings of the prostitution 'of another man' contrary to s 5(1)b of the Sexual Offences Act 1967 (see p 19 f to j, post).

a Section 30 provides:

'(1) It is an offence for a man knowingly to live wholly or in part on the earnings of prostitution.

(2) For the purposes of this section a man who lives with or is habitually in the company of a prostitute, or who exercises control, direction or influence over a prostitute's movements in a way which shows he is aiding, abetting or compelling her prostitution with others, shall be presumed to be knowingly living on the earnings of prostitution, unless he proves the contrary.'

b Section 5(1), so far as material, provides: 'A man or woman who knowingly lives wholly or in part on the earnings of prostitution of another man shall be liable … (b) on conviction on indictment to imprisonment for a term not exceeding seven years.'

Corbett v Corbett (orse Ashley) [1970] 2 All ER 33 applied.

Notes

For the common law offence of keeping a disorderly house, see 11 Halsbury's Laws (4th edn) para 1057, and for cases on the subject, see 15 Digest (Reissue) 1054-1055, 9076-9078.

For living on the earnings of prostitution, see 11 Halsbury's Laws (4th edn) paras 1068, 1070.

For the Sexual Offences Act 1956, s 30, see 8 Halsbury's Statutes (3rd edn) 433.

For the Sexual Offences Act 1967, s 5, see ibid 580.

Cases referred to in judgment

- Corbett v Corbett (orse Ashley) [1970] 2 All ER 33, [1971] P 83, [1970] 2 WLR 1306, 27(1) Digest (Reissue) 29, 137.
- Jenks v Turpin (1884) 13 QBD 505, DC, 8(2) Digest (Reissue) 644, 176.
- R v Berg, Britt, Carr é and Lummies (1927) 20 Cr App R 38, CCA, 14(2) Digest (Reissue) 507, 4150.
- R v Brady, R v Ram [1964] 3 All ER 616, CCA, 15 Digest (Reissue) 1055, 9078.
- R v Higginson (1762) 2 Burr 1232, 97 ER 806, 15 Digest (Reissue) 1055, 9080.
- R v Quinn, R v Bloom [1961] 3 All ER 88, [1962] 2 QB 245, [1961] 3 WLR 611, CCA, 15 Digest (Reissue) 1055, 9077.
- R v Rogier (1823) 2 Dow & Ry KB 431.
- Shaw v DPP [1961] 2 All ER 446, [1962] AC 220, [1961] 2 WLR 897, HL, 14(1) Digest (Reissue) 139, 965.

Appeals and applications for leave to appeal

On 28 September 1982 in the Crown Court at Inner London Sessions, before Mr R U Thomas sitting as an assistant recorder and a jury (1) the appellant Moira Tan was convicted of keeping a disorderly house at 89b Warwick Way, London SW1 (count 1), was sentenced to six months' imprisonment and was deprived of property rights in 13 apparatus found on the premises, (2) the appellant Gloria Gina Greaves was convicted (i) of keeping a disorderly house at 89b Warwick Way, London SW1 (count 1), (ii) of keeping a disorderly house at 15 Clarendon Street, London SW1 (count 2) and (iii) of living on the earnings of prostitution (of the applicant Tan) contrary to s 30 of the Sexual Offences Act 1956 (count 3), was sentenced to six months' imprisonment, concurrent, on counts 1 and 2, and to twelve months' imprisonment, consecutive, on count 3, and was also fined £10,000 on count 3 (or six months' consecutive imprisonment in default of payment) and deprived of property rights in apparatus found at 89b Warwick Way and 15 Clarendon Street, (3) the appellant Brian Greaves was convicted of living on the earnings of prostitution (through his association with Gloria Greaves) contrary to s 30 of the 1956 Act (count 4), and of living on the earnings of male prostitution (of the appellant Gloria Greaves), contrary to s 5 of the Sexual Offence Act 1967 (count 5). Each of the appellants appealed against conviction on points of law. The appellant Tan appealed against sentence by leave of Bush J. The appellants Gloria Greaves and Brian Greaves applied for leave to appeal against sentence. Their applications were referred by Bush J to the full court. The facts are set out in the judgment of the court.

Nicholas Freeman for the appellant Tan.

Andrew Patience for the appellants Gloria Greaves and Brian Greaves.

John P V Bevan for the Crown.

At the conclusion of the hearing of the appeals May LJ announced that for reasons to be given later the court (1) would allow the appeal of Brian Greaves against his conviction on count 4 and would quash that conviction, but that all the other appeals against conviction would be dismissed, (2) would grant the applications for leave to appeal against sentence, treating the hearing as the hearing of the appeals against sentence, and (3) would allow the appeals against sentence inasmuch as all sentences would be suspended for two years.

JUDGMENT

10 February 1983. The following judgment was delivered.

PARKER J. On 28 September 1982 the appellants were convicted in the Crown Court at Inner London Sessions on an indictment containing five counts. On count 1, Tan and Gloria Greaves were convicted of keeping a disorderly house at 89b Warwick Way, London SW1, and were each sentenced to six months' imprisonment. Both were, in addition, deprived of property rights in apparatus found at such premises. On count 2, Gloria Greaves was convicted of keeping a disorderly house at 15 Clarendon Street, London SW1, and was sentenced to six months' imprisonment, concurrent with the sentence on count 1, and was also deprived of property rights in apparatus found there. On count 3, Gloria Greaves was convicted of living on the earnings of prostitution contrary to s 30 of the Sexual Offences Act 1956, and was sentenced to twelve months' imprisonment, consecutive to the sentences imposed on counts 1 and 2, was fined £10,000 or six months' consecutive in default of payment and was ordered to pay the prosecution's costs. The total custodial sentence imposed on her thus amounted to eighteen months' imprisonment. On count 4, Brian Greaves was convicted of living on the earnings of prostitution contrary to s 30 of the 1956 Act, and was sentenced to twelve months' imprisonment. On count 5, Brian Greaves was also convicted of living on the earnings of male prostitution contrary to s 5 of the Sexual Offences Act 1967, and was sentenced to twelve months' imprisonment, concurrent with the sentence on count 4.

All the appellants appealed on points of law. Tan appealed against sentence by leave of the single judge. Applications by Gloria Greaves and Brian Greaves for leave to appeal against sentence were referred by the single judge to the full court. The single judge also granted all three defendants bail, pending the hearing of their appeals and applications.

The appeals against conviction, the appeal against sentence and the applications for leave to appeal against sentence were heard on 7 and 8 December 1982. On the conclusion of the hearing, the appeal of Brian Greaves against his conviction on count 4 was allowed and that conviction was quashed, but all other appeals against conviction were dismissed. 14The applications for leave to appeal against sentence were granted and the hearing treated as the hearing of the appeals against sentence. All the appeals against sentence were allowed, to the extent only that all sentences of imprisonment were suspended for two years. We then said that we would give our reasons later. This we do now. We deal first with counts 1 and 2.

At 89b Warwick Way, Tan, and at 15 Clarendon Street, Gloria Greaves, provided sexual services for reward to those wishing to receive them. Tan rented 89b Warwick Way from Greaves. The services provided were of a like nature in each case. They involved the use of much equipment of a similar kind and were provided in the case of Warwick Way by Tan alone and in the case of Clarendon Street by Gloria Greaves alone. They were provided in private, in that there were no other participants than the client or customer and, in the one case, Tan, and, in the other, Greaves. In no case were there any observers. There might, however, from time to time, be a customer waiting in a neighbouring room whilst a previous customer was in receipt of the services for which he had come to the premises.

The services provided at both premises were of a particularly revolting and perverted kind. Straightforward sexual intercourse was not provided at all. With the aid of a mass of equipment, some manual (such as whips and chains), some mechanical and some electrical, clients were subjected, at their own wish and with their full consent, to a variety of forms of humiliation, flagellation, bondage and torture, accompanied often by masturbation.

The availability of the services provided at both premises was advertised extensively, including by insertion in what are known as 'contact magazines', which are published and available to the public. An example of such an advertisement, in relation to each of the premises, is as follows.

89b Warwick Way:

'Humiliation enthusiast, my favourite pastime is humiliating and disciplining mature male submissives, in strict bondage, lovely tan coloured mistress invites humble applicants, T.V., C.B., B., D. and rubber wear, 12 p.m. to 7 p.m. Mon. to Fri. 89 Basement Flat, Warwick Way, Victoria, SW1.'

15 Clarendon Street:

'The most equipped mistress in Town, report now for C.P., W.S., D.H.N. Racks, stocks, pillory, dungeon, T.V.'s wardrobe, stiletto heels, boots, rubber, leather, E-shocks, Maid training etc. etc. You name it? Madam has it, also madam does nursing treatments, intimate examinations, Victorian and modern enemas. Bottle and breast feeding. Nappy changing by Nanny. Report to Madam Stern, 15 Clarendon Street, Basement Flat, Victoria, London, SW1.'

It will be noted that in these two cases, addresses but not telephone numbers are given. In other cases, there were telephone numbers provided and appointments could be made either by telephone or by going to the premises. The advertisements constitute a clear invitation to any member of the public so inclined to resort to the premises and there submit himself to perverted practices.

At the close of the prosecution case at the trial, it was submitted that there was no case to answer, on the ground that, where a single prostitute provided sexual services to a single client at a time in private in certain premises, such premises were incapable in law of being a disorderly house. That submission was rejected. The case was left to the jury, who duly convicted on both counts. No complaint is made of the summing up and it was indeed accepted that if premises are, despite the fact that the sexual services are always provided to a single client in private, capable of being a disorderly house, then both the premises here in question were virtually certain to be found by a jury to be within that description. The submission made at the trial was repeated before us as the only ground of appeal on counts 1 and 2.

Keeping a disorderly house is a common law offence, albeit that it received limited statutory attention in the Disorderly Houses Act 1751 in two respects, namely, first, that by s 2 places kept for public dancing, music or other public entertainment within or within 20 miles of the cities of London and Westminster were, unless licensed, deemed 15 to be disorderly houses and, second, that by s 5 prosecutions were encouraged against those keeping bawdy-houses, gaming houses or other disorderly houses. We can find little assistance in this Act on the question whether, as was submitted on behalf of the appellants, an essential ingredient of a disorderly house is a plurality of either participants or spectators. Such indication as there is suggests, however, that such plurality is not required. A bawdy-house would clearly cover a house in which two prostitutes operated entirely in separate rooms, never saw more than one client at a time and were never observed by anyone else, and the wording accepts or recognises that a bawdy-house is or may be a disorderly house.

Two early cases were cited in argument, namely *R v Higginson* (1762) 2 Burr 1232, 97 ER 806 and *R v Rogier* (1823) 2 Dow & Ry KB 431. In the first of such cases, a motion in restraint of judgment on the ground that the indictment on which the defendant had been convicted was too general failed, but the court held the indictment good without giving reasons and without hearing argument. The particulars in the indictment certainly alleged that 'certain evil and ill-disposed persons ... come together ... fighting of cocks, boxing, playing at cudgels and misbehaving themselves', but there is nothing to indicate that, had the indictment alleged that a succession of 'evil and ill-disposed persons' had resorted to the premises and there separately and successively indulged with the proprietor in 'cock-fighting, boxing, playing at cudgels and misbehaving', the indictment would have been bad.

R v Rogier (1823) 2 Dow & Ry KB 431 is more helpful. The defendants were convicted of keeping a common gaming house and permitting an unlawful game called 'Rouge et Noir'. As in *R v Higginson*, there was a motion in restraint of judgment. In his judgment Abbott CJ said (at 433):

'If a common gaming house be so conducted that it becomes a receptacle for idle and disorderly persons, who are permitted to assemble there and enter into play for sums of an illegal amount, it becomes a public nuisance, and the maintaining it is an offence indictable at common law; and if the game of "Rouge et Noir," or any other game, however innocent in itself, is played at by such persons, and to an excessive amount, it becomes an illegal game, and those who hold out to others the means of so playing at it are guilty of a common law offence.'

This case is of importance for two reasons. First, it shows that a game innocent in itself may become unlawful if it is played for stakes which a jury consider to be excessive. Second, it contains the plain statement that those who hold out to others the means of playing such a game are guilty of a common law offence. The reference to people being permitted to assemble was said to indicate that a plurality of persons was necessary. In its context, however, we have no doubt that it contains no such indication. It is no more than a reference to the facts of the particular case. We should also mention that, if and in so far as this case appears to indicate that there can be no conviction for keeping a gaming house or indeed other disorderly houses unless there is a public nuisance, it has since been decided that this is unnecessary (see *R v Quinn, R v Bloom* [1961] 3 All ER 88, [1962] 2 QB 245, to which we revert hereafter).

The first case in which the definition of what constitutes a disorderly house was expressly considered was *R v Berg, Britt, Carr é and Lummies* (1927) 20 Cr App R 38. The appellants in that case were convicted of a 'conspiracy to corrupt the morals of and to debauch persons resorting to a certain disorderly house', and two of them were convicted of keeping a disorderly house. The recorder, in directing the jury, had used the definition of 'disorderly' in Webster's Dictionary, namely 'Not regulated by the restraints of morality; unchaste; of bad repute, as a disorderly house'. In his judgment Avory J said (at 41-42):

'The Recorder's definition, from Webster is somewhat vague, but would be correct if the element of keeping open house is present and there is added "being so conducted as to violate law and good order." ... The argument that unless the house is open to the public at large its disorderliness is not indictable is refuted by *Rogier* ((1823) 2 Dow & Ry KB 431) cited by Hawkins J. in *Jenks v. Turpin* ((1884) 13 QBD 16505): those cases referred to gaming houses, but the decisions equally apply to the practices here in question ... The gist of the indictment was that the accused were lewd and immoral persons assembled for the purpose of unnatural practices.'

The facts of the case are not set out in the report, but it may be inferred that the accused and others took part in exhibitions of a perverted nature for the edification of those resorting to the premises. The case provides clear authority that (a) there must be some element of keeping open house, albeit the premises need not be open to the public at large, (b) the house must not be regulated by the restraints of morality, or must be unchaste or of bad repute, and (c) it must be so conducted as to violate law and good order.

The definition of disorderly house was further considered in *R v Quinn, R v Bloom* [1961] 3 All ER 88, [1962] 2 QB 245. The premises there in question were used for the performance of acts of strip-tease, some of which acts were, on the evidence, seriously indecent and, in some respects, revolting. The appellants were convicted of keeping a disorderly house and the convictions were upheld. The court, subject to two comments, accepted a definition which was advanced by the prosecution and derived, at least in part, from observations of the House of Lords in *Shaw v DPP* [1961] 2 All ER 446, [1962] AC 220. That definition was in the following terms ([1961] 3 All ER 88 at 91, [1962] 2 QB 245 at 255):

'A disorderly house is a house conducted contrary to law and good order in that matters are performed or exhibited of such a character that their performance or exhibition in a place of common resort (a) amounts to an outrage of public decency or (b) tends to corrupt or deprave or (c) is otherwise calculated to injure the public interest so as to call for condemnation and punishment.'

The two comments made by the court were, first, that the essence of the charge in that case was that indecent performances had taken place, and that the charge might be based on some other ground. The definition must therefore be taken as limited to cases in which indecent exhibitions are alleged. Second, although the elements specified in (a), (b) and (c) of the definition were expressed as alternatives, they should not be regarded as mutually exclusive.

In addition to accepting, subject to the two comments, the definition advanced by the prosecution, the court also rejected in short shrift both the argument that a public nuisance was a necessary ingredient of the offence and the argument that, since those resorting to the premises did not themselves take part in any indecent behaviour, the premises could not be a disorderly house.

The last case to which it is necessary to refer is *R v Brady, R v Ram* [1964] 3 All ER 616, where the court accepted without deciding that, in order to constitute the common law offence of keeping a disorderly house, some element of persistent use was required.

If the definition in *R v Berg, Britt, Carr é and Lummies* is taken, there can be no doubt that there was evidence in the present case on which the jury could find that the premises were in each case not regulated by the restraints of morality. It is said, however, that it was not so conducted as to violate law and good order, since what took place between the defendants and each client was not itself a criminal offence and that there was not the necessary element of open house.

Both contentions we reject. A strip-tease performance is not itself a criminal offence, but *R v Quinn, R v Bloom* shows that it may so overpass what is acceptable, that it may become unlawful just as gaming may be excessive and thus unlawful. It is for the jury to set the standard. As to the element of open house, there was clearly a public invitation to resort to the premises for the purpose of indulging in perverted and revolting practices. This invitation by advertisement was equally clearly part of the conduct of the premises, and we have no doubt that it was open to the jury to find both that this constituted a sufficient element of open house and that, as a result, the premises were conducted in violation of law and good order.

In *Shaw v DPP* [1961] 2 All ER 446 at 460, [1962] AC 220 at 281 Lord Reid, in his minority opinion, said: 17

'The evidence shows that the invitations were to resort to certain of the prostitutes for the purpose of certain forms of perversion. That I would think to be an offence for a different reason ... the authorities ... establish that it is an indictable offence to say or do or exhibit anything in public which outrages public decency ... In my view, it is open to a jury to hold that a public invitation to indulge in sexual perversion does so outrage public decency as to be a punishable offence.'

Lord Reid was not prepared to go as far as other members of the House of Lords but, even on the basis of his minority opinion, it would have been open to the jury to hold that the advertisements in the present case alone constituted an offence and thus that the premises were conducted contrary to law and good order.

Turning to the definition in *R v Quinn, R v Bloom*, it clearly cannot be applied in terms to the present case, for here there were no performances or exhibitions as such. If, however, *R v Berg, Britt, Carr é and Lummies,* and *R v Quinn, R v Bloom* are taken together, in the light of what was said in *Shaw v DPP*, we have no hesitation in rejecting the submission made. Were it correct, it would mean that it would be open to anyone (so long as perverted practices were conducted with one client at a time) to advertise such services without restriction, no matter how revolting they might be, thereby encouraging the public to indulge in them and to allow others (so long as they did not observe or take part) to await their turn to partake of such practices.

No doubt a prosecution in circumstances like the present is novel. It was submitted that the trend is for the criminal law to withdraw from concern with what takes place between consenting adults in private (with the single exception of buggery between a man and a woman) and that the courts should not create a new offence. We accept that the prosecution is novel, that the courts should not or should at least be slow to create new offences and that the tendency alleged exists. Novelty is, however, no valid objection (see *Berg* and *Shaw*) and to reject the submission is not to create a new offence but to hold that a certain set of circumstances, not hitherto made the subject of the charge, fall squarely within the scope of an existing offence.

In *Quinn* the court did not seek to lay down an exhaustive definition. Nor do we. Many forms of conduct may fall within the scope of the offence, and to attempt to establish a universal definition with precision is both undesirable and impossible. It is, however, both desirable and possible to indicate how a jury should be directed, where the ground on which the charge is based is that the premises are being used for the provision of sexual services. In such cases, the direction, adapting the definition in *R v Quinn, R v Bloom* [1961] 3 All ER 88 at 91, [1962] 2 QB 245 at 255, would in our judgment be that, in order to convict, the jury must be satisfied that the services provided are open to those members of the public who wish to partake of them and are of such a character and are conducted in such a manner (whether by advertisement or otherwise) that their provision amounts to an outrage of public decency or is otherwise calculated to injure the public interest to such an extent as to call for condemnation and punishment. They should further be directed that the fact, if it be a fact, that the services are provided by a single prostitute to one client at a time and without spectators does not prevent the house being a disorderly house.

Finally, with regard to the appeal on counts 1 and 2, we observe that acceptance of the submission would involve results that fly in the face of common sense. Premises would, for example, be incapable of being a disorderly house if there was a large notice in neon lights over the door containing an open invitation to be whipped or subjected to any form of perversion, with the tariff set out. Yet the law would be powerless to intervene, save, perhaps, under the Indecent Displays (Control) Act 1981, so long as the service itself was provided successively to those resorting to the premises and this would be so, notwithstanding that the adjoining premises had similar notices and provided similar services. To hold that the law was powerless in such a case, but could act in the case of a much more discreet invitation so long as there was in addition to the prostitute and her client a watcher or watchers, offends against common sense.

In *Shaw v DPP* [1961] 2 All ER 446 at 453, [1962] AC 220 at 268 Viscount Simonds said:

'Let it be supposed that at some future, perhaps, early, date homosexual practices 18 between adult consenting males are no longer a crime. Would it not be an offence if, even without obscenity, such practices were publicly advocated and encouraged by pamphlet and advertisement? Or must we wait until Parliament finds time to deal with such conduct? I say, my Lords, that if the common law is powerless in such an event, then we should no longer do her reverence.'

It may well be that in the circumstances supposed by Viscount Simonds a jury would not now convict, but it is for the jury and not the judges to decide whether conduct exceeds the limits of what, at any period of time, is acceptable. For the judges to adopt the stance that no matter how it may be advertised or provided anything, except heterosexual buggery, is permissible between consenting adults in private would be for the judges partially to usurp the functions of juries. The judges' task is to determine whether conduct is capable of being a crime. It is for the jury to decide in an individual case whether it is.

In the case of the two counts presently under consideration, the recorder rightly decided that it was open to the jury to convict. On the evidence, the jury did convict and it could not be and was not suggested that, if the legal submission failed, there was otherwise than ample evidence to justify the convictions in both cases.

For the above reasons, the appeals on counts 1 and 2 were dismissed.

An essential ingredient of the offences charged in counts 3 and 5 was that Gloria Greaves was a man. It was accepted that Gloria Greaves was born a man and remained biologically a man, albeit he had undergone both hormone and surgical treatment, consisting in what are called 'sex change operations', consisting essentially in the removal of the external male organs and the creation of an artificial vaginal pocket.

In *Corbett v Corbett (orse Ashley)* [1970] 2 All ER 33, [1971] P 83 it was held that a person who was born a man and remained biologically a man was a man for the purposes of marriage, and thus that a form of marriage between a man and another person born a man was a nullity, no matter that such last-mentioned person had undergone operative and other sex change treatment.

It was, however, contended that for the purposes of s 30 of the Sexual Offences Act 1956 and s 5 of the Sexual Offences Act 1967 another test should be applied; that, if the person had become philosophically or psychologically or socially female, that person should be held not to be a man for the purposes of the sections and that, on this basis, the evidence was inconclusive and the counts ought to have been withdrawn from the jury.

We reject this submission without hesitation. In our judgment, both common sense and the desirability of certainty and consistency demand that the decision in *Corbett v Corbett* should apply for the purpose, not only of marriage, but also for a charge under s 30 of the Sexual Offences Act 1956 or s 5 of the Sexual Offences Act 1967. The same test would apply also if a man had indulged in buggery with another biological man. That the Corbett v Corbett decision would apply in such a case was accepted on behalf of the appellant. It would, in our view, create an unacceptable situation if the law were such that a marriage between Gloria Greaves and another man was a nullity, on the ground that Gloria Greaves was a man; that buggery to which she consented with such other person was not an offence for the same reason; but that Gloria Greaves could live on the earnings of a female prostitute without offending against s 30 of the 1956 Act because for that purpose he/she was not a man and that the like position would arise in the case of someone charged with living on his earnings as a male prostitute.

A further ground of appeal was raised in relation to count 3, namely that the jury were incorrectly, or insufficiently, directed as to the ingredients of the offence. As to this we need say no more than that having carefully considered the summing up we can discern no insufficiency of directions or any misdirection. The appeals on counts 3 and 5 were accordingly dismissed.

There remained, so far as the convictions were concerned, only the appeal of Brian Greaves against his conviction on count 4, which was allowed. We can deal with this very shortly.

When directing the jury on this count, the recorder stated initially that the prosecution relied on the presumption in s 30(2) of the Sexual Offences Act 1956. This was not in fact the case. The recorder mistakenly thought that count 4 charged Greaves with living on 19 the earnings of Gloria Greaves and thus that the presumption would arise if he was living with Gloria Greaves or was habitually in the latter's company. He carefully and properly directed the jury as to the effect of the section and the burden of proof, but it was then pointed out to him by the prosecution that count 4 did not relate to Brian Greaves living on the earnings of Gloria Greaves, but of Tan and another prostitute, with neither of whom was he living, and thus that no question of a presumption under s 30(2) arose. The recorder then withdrew his direction to the jury with regard to that subsection, but gave no further direction, other than to say that the prosecution had to prove everything.

We are satisfied that, on withdrawal of his earlier direction, the recorder should, however shortly, have reminded the jury of the precise matters of which they had to be satisfied before they could convict Greaves of living on the earnings of either Tan or the other prostitute. In the absence of such a direction, the jury may well have been left in a state of some confusion and uncertainty. This being so, the verdict on this count could only be regarded as unsafe and unsatisfactory. It follows, therefore, that the conviction had to be quashed.

We turn now to the sentences. Apart from the custodial sentences, no point was pressed before us and we do not, therefore, find it necessary to deal with the orders for deprivation of property rights against Tan and Gloria Greaves, or the £10,000 fine and costs awarded against Gloria Greaves. We need only say that they were fully justified. As to the custodial sentences, we have no doubt that custodial sentences of the lengths imposed were also fully justified. Indeed, they exhibit a degree of leniency, no doubt flowing from the fact that in the case of Tan and Gloria Greaves they genuinely believed that they were not offending against the law. We considered, however, that the uncertainties in the law justified the exercise of further leniency and that it would be appropriate to suspend the sentences. It should, however, be known that in the case of others offending in like manner immediate custodial sentences of greater length can be expected.

In the case of Brian Greaves the position is different. He was undoubtedly living on the earnings of Gloria Greaves, whether a man or a woman, and can have been in no doubt on the subject. On the other hand, on count 5, which is the only conviction against him which survives and the only charge of living on the earnings of Gloria Greaves, it is said and we accept, first, that he had gone through a ceremony of marriage with and regarded Gloria Greaves as a female and, second, that there was no element of coercion involved. This being so, we considered it right in this case also to suspend the sentence.

This judgment and the sentences likely to be imposed in the future will, we hope, serve as a warning to others that to invite the public to resort to premises and there indulge in conduct going beyond the limits which a jury regard as tolerable is criminal conduct, even if those responding are attended to in succession and in private, and that such criminal conduct may well result in immediate custodial sentences.

All appeals against conviction dismissed with the exception of Brian Greaves's appeal against his conviction on count 4, which was allowed. All appeals against sentence allowed to the extent that all the sentences of imprisonment were suspended for two years.

The court refused leave to appeal to the House of Lords but extended, under s 34 of the Criminal Appeal Act 1968, the time in which application for leave to appeal might be made to the House by 14 days and certified, under s 33(2) of that Act, that the following point of law of general public importance was involved in the decision: whether premises could be a disorderly house, notwithstanding that every sexual act that took place therein was between a single prostitute and a single customer unobserved by any other person.

14 April. The Appeal Committee of the House of Lords (Lord Diplock, Lord Bridge of Harwich and Lord Brandon of Oakbrook) dismissed petitions by the appellants Tan, Gloria Greaves and Brian Greaves for leave to appeal.

Solicitors: Coles & Stevenson (for the appellant Tan); Knapp-Fishers (for the appellants Gloria Greaves and Brian Greaves); D M O'Shea (for the Crown)

Nothing Like a Dame

The Scandals of Shirley Porter

ANDREW HOSKEN

Granta Books
London

Rodney Hylton-Potts. Lewis still refuses to talk about his links to the two men, although there was nothing illegal about the deal they would strike.

Whybrow, according to Hylton-Potts, was a qualified barrister and 'a very, very remarkable dealer. Beak nose. Violent mood swings. He could be very amusing and then suddenly turn. An extraordinary character. But very, very shrewd.' Despite his talents, Whybrow was not flourishing at the time, and as Hylton-Potts puts it, 'Whybrow hadn't got a pot to piss in.' He looked successful and was living in a six-bedroom house in St John's Wood where he threw big parties, but in fact rented the house for £400 a year thanks to a cheap tenancy under rent legislation.

Just as Lewis was agreeing the exchange of contracts with the City Council, Whybrow visited Hylton-Potts's offices at Cheval Place in South Kensington. Hylton-Potts recalls, 'He came to see me one day and said, "We've got a very good deal." He said he had bought three cemeteries from a man called Clive Lewis.' Neither Hylton-Potts nor Whybrow could at first believe that Westminster was selling off the freeholds, allowing a purchaser to dispose of the graveyards in any way he saw fit. It was the height of irresponsibility by Westminster, but it had the makings of a very profitable deal.

Whybrow agreed to buy the cemeteries once he had found someone to whom they could be sold. He knew they had no financial value, but things might be different if they were part of a business package which included a huge incentive to any prospective buyer. Lewis was keeping the valuable assets such as the properties and the crematorium freehold for himself, but was prepared to sell the twelve acres of undeveloped grazing land, known as Milespit Hill, adjoining Mill Hill cemetery.

Also technically worthless, Milespit Hill was designated Green Belt land and Barnet council was unlikely to allow houses to be built there, but if the council changed its mind, the land would be worth an estimated £5.5 million. Whybrow's aim was to convince a buyer that there was a possibility that Barnet would allow homes to be built on Milespit Hill. The purchaser would have to take the cemeteries as well, but it was under no legal obligation to maintain them because the covenant would not be binding. Whybrow thought buyers would be convinced by the deal if he could tell them he was acting as a 'receiver' to a company which owned the cemeteries, and that his job was to sell them off. 'People think, "receivership; fire-sale: cheap",' says Hylton-Potts bluffly. Hylton-Potts purchased a company, based in Panama, called Chelwood Holdings, to pose as the company in receivership. He recalls, 'I picked Chelwood Holdings for Whybrow quite by chance. It was a nice name. Unbeknownst to any of us, Lady Porter lived in Chelwood House and had a company called Chelwood Nominees. I'd never met Lady Porter, Whybrow never met Lady Porter. But the press later got hold of it and thought it must be Lady Porter! It's as simple as that. Had I chosen "Bloggs Holdings" there would have been much less shit. Pure chance!'

Whybrow now just needed a buyer. He told an inquiry in 1988, 'We hit what we thought were the eight major companies, and excuse the expression, in the "death business". The response came back: "No interest at all, we think it's absolutely worthless." As for the maintenance agreement,' remembered Whybrow, 'I don't think anybody bothered with it.' In the course of his business ventures Whybrow met a mysterious Swedish businessman who lived behind high security fences in a mansion at Bourne End in Hertfordshire. And, because he was a Swede, Whybrow and Hylton-Potts knew him simply as 'The Turnip'. In December 1986, seven months after Lewis exchanged contracts with Westminster, Whybrow had concluded a different property deal in Islington with the Turnip, and the pair went for a drink in the Loose Box wine bar in Cheval Place. 'Have you got anything else, Whybrow?' asked the Turnip. 'No,' replied Whybrow. 'It's a bit quiet really. I've got three bloody cemeteries.' The Turnip asked if he could have a look at them. Whybrow demurred, 'I'm awfully sorry but you're a bit late.' The Turnip pressed on, 'Well I have overseas clients who are desperate to get money into this country, please give me a chance.' Whybrow did not ask the Turnip why his clients were desperate to get money into the UK and why more orthodox avenues were denied to them; it was probably wise not to. He simply reiterated, 'Look you're wasting your time.' Brilliantly, Whybrow further tempted the Turnip by offering to sell him Milespit Hill. For the

Turnip, the graveyards and the twelve acres of grazing land made a good package: his clients could get their money into the country; there was no legal obligation to maintain the cemeteries, and Milespit Hill would be worth a fortune if Barnet Council ever granted planning permission to build houses.

The Turnip planned to purchase the cemeteries from Whybrow for £1.25 million, through Wisland, one his companies based in Switzerland. Whybrow also sold Milespit Hill to Wisland, sold by Westminster to Clive Lewis for five pence, reportedly for £1.75 million. Whybrow stood to gain £500,000 from the sale of the cemeteries and an extra £100,000 from the grazing land; according to Hylton-Potts, the rest of the profit passed down the line to Lewis. Hylton-Potts was struck by how desperate the Turnip was for the deal. 'He couldn't wait to exchange and complete early,' says Hylton-Potts. 'The Swede was so frightened of losing the deal. He thought it was a good deal for him. And he had no idea that Chelwood didn't own it. He didn't know they'd just owned it for a day; and that was the skill in the deal.' Shortly before completing the deal with the Turnip, Whybrow took fleeting possession of the cemeteries. At ten o'clock one Sunday evening, a taxi drew up outside his house in St John's Wood. The cab driver handed Whybrow an envelope. 'Here mate, these are for you.' Inside were the keys to the three cemeteries.

In April 1986 the council had exchanged contracts with Lewis, but the deal had not been completed. Completion took place nine months later, at the end of January 1987, between businesses such as Whybrow and Wisland of whom the council had no knowledge. Lewis had handed the cemeteries to Royel Investments (Growish Ltd), his parents' dissolved company, which in turn had passed them on to Cemetery Assets Management Ltd, another shell company, whose company secretary was Rodney Hylton-Potts, and whose directors were 'associates' of Whybrow. Cemetery Assets had agreed to sell them on to Chelwood Holdings, whose receiver was Whybrow, which had in turn agreed to sell them on to the Turnip's Wisland company. Contracts were exchanged and completed on the same day among the various parties, and ownership of the cemeteries passed like a greased rugby ball down the line of four offshore companies. Whybrow constructed the deal 'back to back' to pay off Lewis once the Turnip had signed for £1.25 million. Operating as Chelwood, Whybrow used the money he received from Wisland to buy the cemeteries off Cemetery Assets for £750,000 and pocketed the £500,000 difference. Hylton-Potts believes the bulk of the profit went to the inscrutable Lewis but Lewis refuses to comment on the details of the deal. On the same day, the council lost any control it might have had over the welfare of the graveyards, and Porter was completely at the mercy of the mysterious businessmen who now owned them. Wisland promptly abandoned the cemeteries to the elements and the fly-tippers and submitted plans to build houses on Milespit Hill.

To celebrate his triumph, John Whybrow treated himself to a holiday at the Monte Rosa Hotel in Zermatt, Switzerland. He paid the pianist at the bar to play Tchaikovsky's *Funeral March* over and over again, and tipped him each time. It was only later that he realised he had made a mistake over the exchange rates and had paid the pianist £10 each time instead of £1. He just laughed, flush with money. Later, he bought himself a villa in Spain.

In 1996 John Whybrow and his solicitor, Rodney Hylton-Potts, were jailed at Southwark Crown Court for swindling two Scottish banks. They had used an offshore company to purchase three Scottish hotels, conned the banks into lending more money than they were worth and pocketed the difference. The company was called 'Magus Inns', a play on the words 'major sins', according to the Prosecution. Both men spent two years in jail, after which Hylton-Potts earned national notoriety by winning a television programme called *Vote for Me*, in which he called for a total ban on all immigration and the castration of convicted paedophiles. In the 2005 general election, he stood as a candidate for his Get Britain Back Party in Folkestone against the Conservative leader, Michael Howard, and polled 153 votes. Hylton-Potts last heard that Whybrow had fallen on hard times and was living in a bedsit in Surrey.

In February 1945 the first Town Clerk of the old City of Westminster, Sir John Hunt, had died at the age of eighty-five. The City Fathers and their officials held a memorial service at

photo © Andrew Ward/reportphotos.com

It's WAR! Cemetery relatives protest outside Marylebone Council House.

old music hall number 'Oh Mr Porter!': 'Oh Lady Porter, what will you do? You've promised to buy back the cemeteries, but we don't believe it's true. Give us that inquiry, the public one we'd like, or in 1990, we'll tell you "On yer bike".' But there were major problems with Porter's buy-back plan: how to do it and for how much? Clive Lewis, Rodney Hylton-Potts and John Whybrow were completely untouchable. The deal had been legal and so cleverly orchestrated that none of the speculators could be held accountable. By now, Lewis, the original architect of the deal, had sold the elegant lodge at Hanwell cemetery for £170,000 and there were rumours that the gatehouse at Mill Hill would fetch £300,000, but he had decided to rent it out instead, along with the one at East Finchley. He would also receive £250,000 for the crematorium at East Finchley. As the scandal unravelled, Porter sent out an instruction: 'Nail Clive Lewis.' She never could – and she never did.

Shirley Porter was at the mercy of the mysterious Turnip and his company Wisland. They owned the freehold and, as predicted by class distinction of the characters by dressing the Conservatives in well-tailored business suits with Tory women in pearls and floral frocks while many Labour councillors conveyed their proletarian credentials in sweaters, jeans and open-necked shirts.' During the meeting itself, 'absurdity piled upon absurdity like so many custard pies being flung by drunken clowns'. He described an address by the relatives: 'Their spokesman, pounding the table with the resolution of a scolding headmaster, spoke of foxes having a field day because graves were dug only two and a half feet deep and of the distress of relatives who had come across bones on the overgrown paths.' As for Porter, Shulman said she was 'no sleep-walking Lady Macbeth washing the blood of guilt from her hands' but a tough leader who resolved that 'appropriate action would be taken after several inquiries had been held, negligence of council officers or advisers would be disclosed, serious misjudgements would be reported'.

Paul Foot was the first reporter to name John Whybrow as one of those involved and appealed for help in tracking him down. The council, also desperate to find out what had happened, located him and he consented to an interview in the office of his lawyer, Rodney Hylton-Potts. Whybrow appears to have enjoyed the experience, and still claimed to be a receiver for the worthless Chelwood Holdings Company; he said he had simply disposed of the assets of a company which was in receivership. He told Phillips's inquiry nothing of the quick fortune he had made selling the cemeteries or how the receivership had simply been a ruse to disguise reality. 'I am here to help, sir, as I always have been,' Whybrow said courteously. He then admonished the men from the council: 'It was not our decision, it was yours. I am a Westminster ratepayer and aggrieved at the situation. I don't believe you had any right to sell these cemeteries in the first place. You cannot sell people that have served this community in two world wars.' Phillips and his team were left none the wiser from their encounter with Whybrow. Hylton-Potts says, 'Of course, in reality, Whybrow couldn't give a stuff.'

Until the cemeteries fiasco, Porter had been lionised by the media as the hyper-efficient and no-nonsense Tesco heiress who

FRASER MARR

Court of Appeal (The Lord Chief Justice, Mr. Justice Kennedy and Mr. Justice Hutchison): June 13, 1989

Trial—Conduct of Trial Judge—Entitlement of Defendant to Fair Trial.

It is an inherent principle of the system of trial in England that however distasteful the offence, however repulsive the defendant, however laughable his defence, he is entitled to have his case fairly presented to the jury both by counsel and the trial judge.

The appellant was convicted of indecently assaulting a girl aged 19. The prosecution case was that he had come up behind the complainant and put his hand up between her thighs and squeezed her private parts. The appellant had denied this, maintaining the assault had been accidental. He appealed on three main grounds—(a) during cross-examination the appellant was asked to step down from the witness box and give a demonstration of how the incident had occurred, and the trial judge had refused to allow his counsel to adopt the same form of demonstration procedure during his re-examination; (b) the judge had directed the jury that previous good character could never be a defence to a criminal charge; and (c) that the judge directed the jury that "a furtive little crime of this kind" was not a thing that people tell their friends about or they know about; but by all means give weight to the good reputation he bears amongst his friends and family.

Held, allowing the appeal, that (1) the judge was plainly wrong in inhibiting the defence by his "blanket" refusal to allow the same procedure to be adopted in re-examination as in cross-examination for the same facility should be allowed to the defence as had been properly allowed to the prosecution.

(2) The judge was telling the jury what good character in the appellant could not do, nowhere did he go on to say what good character could do. The jury should have been directed that good character went primarily to credibility, *i.e.* to whether the appellant should be believed or not.

(3) The judge's remarks about a furtive little crime, etc., spoken as it was against the background of the letters from friends and acquaintances who thought highly of the appellant, suggested to the jury that the appellant was a man who was very likely to possess a good reputation, one which he did not deserve.

(4) Thus, as the Court did not think that the appellant's case, however unattractive it might have been, was given the balanced treatment and consideration which was its due, the conviction would have to be quashed for the case was not one for the application of the proviso to section 2(1) of the Criminal Appeal Act 1968.

Appeal against conviction.

On January 19, 1989, in the Crown Court at Middlesex Guild hall (Judge Norwood) the appellant was convicted of indecent assault and was sentenced to 21 days' imprisonment and ordered to pay £475 prosecution costs. The facts appear in the judgment, as do the relevant grounds of appeal.

Robert W. Grey (assigned by the Registrar of Criminal Appeals) for the appellant.

Michael Haynes for the Crown.

THE LORD CHIEF JUSTICE: On January 19, 1989 in the Crown Court at Middlesex Guildhall this appellant, Fraser Marr, aged 27, was convicted of indecent assault. He was sentenced to 21 days' imprisonment and ordered to pay a sum in respect of the prosecution costs.

He now appeals by the leave of this Court which we give, the application for leave having been referred to us by the single judge. Consequently this becomes the hearing of the appeal. He appeals against both conviction and sentence.

The prosecution case was this. The complainant, a 19-year-old girl, who was wearing a sweater, jodhpurs and a jacket, was shortly before 1 o'clock in the afternoon of September 19, 1988, walking along Regent Street. What she said was this. When the appellant, whom she had never seen or met before, overtook her from behind, he crossed so sharply over her path that she was forced to stop. He then pushed his right hand between her legs and with his upturned hand squeezed her private parts. Then he withdrew his hand and walked off as if nothing had happened.

There is no doubt that in her view, and she was obviously an honest witness, that is what had happened. Indeed angered by that she called out to him, "Come back." But when he saw her running towards him, he ran off as fast as he possibly could. She was assisted by a public spirited man who joined in the chase. Neither she nor this man could catch the appellant.

However a police officer in uniform was at hand and he too took up the chase and eventually succeeded in catching the appellant. This was Police Constable Johnson. He said that the appellant did not stop, even though he turned round several times. He must have seen the officer chasing him. It was only when he was grabbed by the jacket that he did stop. He said to the officer, "I've done nothing. Please let me go."

He was then taken back to the complainant and the officer asked the complainant to say what had happened. She then related in the presence of the appellant what she said had happened. The appellant was then arrested, was cautioned and taken to the police station.

He was formally interviewed, and during that formal interview he said he thought that the girl was someone he knew. She resembled a Miss Luxton, who was a friend of the appellant's, and he said he decided accordingly to catch up with her. As he passed by her, intending to turn, face her, walk backwards and have a conversation with her, he reached out, but at that moment realised it was not Miss Luxton at all. His outstretched hand had accidentally, according to him, hit her in the vaginal area and then, because the girl looked very upset, he panicked and ran away. That was his version of events during the formal interview.

He gave evidence at the trial. He said it was lunch time. He was on his way to get some tickets for a theatre. Because he saw his friend Laura Luxton walking in front of him, he decided to catch her up. It was his intention to pass by her and then whilst facing her walk backwards, and exchange a few words before he continued on his way. When he drew alongside her, just as he was about to turn his face, he suddenly realised it was not Laura Luxton at all. At that very moment he happened to be on the kerb and he lost his footing. In order to regain his balance he reached out with his right hand, and his hand accidentally went between the girl's thighs. He said he did not squeeze her private parts. As he withdrew his hand it did press against them and that may have appeared to her to be like a squeeze. He was very embarrassed, and he decided it was best to leave rapidly and not to make matters any worse. Hence the running away.

Miss Luxton was called by the defence. There was a resemblance in the hair style between the complainant and Miss Luxton, but there was a difference in their heights and also a difference between their physical configuration.

Some 20 character references were also submitted to the court. Eight of the references were read.

The jury retired at 11.30 and came back at 1 o'clock to return their unanimous verdict.

Those very briefly were the facts.

The appellant complains that the learned judge conducted the case in such a way that the appellant was not, to put it bluntly, given a fair run.

No one could doubt that if the allegations made by the prosecution were true, this was a singularly unattractive crime, earning the offender no sort of sympathy. Likewise the nature of the defence was, to say the very least, most unimpressive. It is however an inherent principle of our system of trial that however distasteful the offence, however repulsive the defendant, however laughable his defence, he is nevertheless entitled to have his case fairly presented to the jury both by counsel and by the judge. Indeed it is probably true to say that it is just in those cases where the cards seem to be stacked most heavily against the defendant that the judge should be most scrupulous to ensure that nothing untoward takes place which might exacerbate the defendant's difficulties.

The appellant contends through Mr. Grey, his counsel, that the conduct of this trial fell short of those ideals to such an extent that however unlikely the defendant's story might have been, nevertheless this Court should intervene. Mr. Grey has gone through thoroughly and properly a large number of complaints about the way the learned judge conducted this trial.

There are however three main grounds upon which he places particular reliance. They are these. First of all during the course of cross-examination the appellant was asked to step down from the witness box and to give a demonstration of how it was that he said the incident had taken place. When the time came for re-examination, the judge refused to allow Mr. Grey to adopt the same form of demonstration procedure. It is true that Mr Grey asked that it might be done with a model, a matter which the judge would have been right in our judgment to decline. But that was not the basis of the judge's refusal. It was a "blanket" refusal, if I may use that expression, to allow the same procedure to be adopted in re-examination as had been allowed in cross-examination.

The judge, in our view, was clearly wrong to inhibit the defence in this way. The same facility should have been allowed to the defence as had been properly allowed to the prosecution.

Secondly complaint is made about the way in which the judge dealt with the question of character. The appellant was a man who had never been in trouble with the law before. It was the case, as our short résumé of the facts may have indicated, where much turned on the credibility of the evidence given by the appellant himself.

The judge's directions on this matter are in these terms:

> "It is my duty to say this to you: being of good character—by which we mean having no previous convictions and being highly thought of by his friends—can never be a defence to a criminal charge. We are, all of us, born into this world without previous convictions. Most of us hope to leave it in the same state. If, however, there is to be a conviction, there is going to be a first time. You can get somebody in that dock—and believe me, you do—with forty previous convictions. There was a time when that person did say to a judge and jury, 'I have no previous convictions.' So it can never be a defence to a criminal charge."

The learned judge should, in our judgment, have directed the jury that good character goes primarily to credibility, to whether the defendant should be believed by the jury or not. But it also has a further significance as explained in the decision of this Court in *Bryant and Oxley* (1978) 67 Cr.App.R. 157, 165, (1978) 2 All E.R. 689, 695.

This matter was made clear in the recent decision of another division of this Court, *Berrada* , *The Times*, February 20, 1989, C.A. It was a decision which came after the date of the instant trial. So it could not have been before the learned judge during the course of the instant trial. It was in fact an appeal from the same judge who had used very similar words to those which I have just read.

Waterhouse J. delivering the judgment of the Court in *Berrada* had this to say, having read out the passage about which complaint was made:

> "The striking omission in that passage is of any reference to the real and primary relevance of the appellant's previous good character. What the learned judge should have said was that it was primarily relevant to the question of the appellant's credibility. Moreover, this was clearly a case in which questions of credibility went to the heart of the matters that the jury had to decide, subject to the qualification that the burden of proof remained throughout on the prosecution. There was a decisive conflict of evidence between the complainant and the appellant and between him and the police so that it was necessary that the jury should be given proper guidance in relation to the appellant's credibility.
>
> In the judgment of this Court, the appellant was entitled to have put to the jury from the judge herself a correct direction about the relevance of his previous good character to his credibility. That is a conventional direction and it is regrettable that it did not appear in the summing up in this case. It would have been proper also (but was not obligatory) for the judge to refer to the fact that the previous good character of the appellant might be thought by them to be one relevant factor when they were considering whether he was the kind of man who was likely to have behaved in the way that the prosecution alleged."

The judge, in the passage which we have read from her direction to the jury, was telling the jury what good character in the defendant cannot do, but nowhere did she go on to say what good character can do. The two items which she should have mentioned were set out by Waterhouse J. in the case of *Berrada* which we have just cited.

The third matter on which Mr. Grey relies is a passage which follows on immediately after the passage which I have read relating to character. It reads as follows:

> "The furtive little crime of this kind is not the kind of thing that people tend to tell their friends about, or that their friends would be likely to know about. However that may be, by all means give weight to the good reputation that he bears amongst his friends and family."

That expression starting with the "The furtive little crime" is certainly capable, to say the least, of meaning that this is the sort of crime which a man may be committing regularly without any of his friends or acquaintances knowing about it. Indeed it is a little difficult to see what other interpretation can be put upon those words.

Spoken as that passage was against the background of what the judge described as "an inordinate number of letters from friends and acquaintances who think very highly of him," it may, and almost certainly did, suggest to the jury that here was a man who may have been very lucky to possess a good reputation, one which he may not have deserved.

Those were the three main points upon which Mr. Grey on behalf of the appellant relied in his argument. There were a number of other complaints about the nature of this trial, and the way in which the judge conducted it, into which we do not deem it necessary to go.

The cumulative effect of all the matters raised by Mr. Grey was such, in the view

Some 20 character references were also submitted to the court. Eight of the references were read.

The jury retired at 11.30 and came back at 1 o'clock to return their unanimous verdict.

Those very briefly were the facts.

The appellant complains that the learned judge conducted the case in such a way that the appellant was not, to put it bluntly, given a fair run.

No one could doubt that if the allegations made by the prosecution were true, this was a singularly unattractive crime, earning the offender no sort of sympathy. Likewise the nature of the defence was, to say the very least, most unimpressive. It is however an inherent principle of our system of trial that however distasteful the offence, however repulsive the defendant, however laughable his defence, he is nevertheless entitled to have his case fairly presented to the jury both by counsel and by the judge. Indeed it is probably true to say that it is just in those cases where the cards seem to be stacked most heavily against the defendant that the judge should be most scrupulous to ensure that nothing untoward takes place which might exacerbate the defendant's difficulties.

The appellant contends through Mr. Grey, his counsel, that the conduct of this trial fell short of those ideals to such an extent that however unlikely the defendant's story might have been, nevertheless this Court should intervene. Mr. Grey has gone through thoroughly and properly a large number of complaints about the way the learned judge conducted this trial.

There are however three main grounds upon which he places particular reliance. They are these. First of all during the course of cross-examination the appellant was asked to step down from the witness box and to give a demonstration of how it was that he said the incident had taken place. When the time came for re-examination, the judge refused to allow Mr. Grey to adopt the same form of demonstration procedure. It is true that Mr. Grey asked that it might be done with a model, a matter which the judge would have been right in our judgment to decline. But that was not the basis of the judge's refusal. It was a "blanket" refusal, if I may use that expression, to allow the same procedure to be adopted in re-examination as had been allowed in cross-examination.

The judge, in our view, was clearly wrong to inhibit the defence in this way. The same facility should have been allowed to the defence as had been properly allowed to the prosecution.

Secondly complaint is made about the way in which the judge dealt with the question of character. The appellant was a man who had never been in trouble with the law before. It was the case, as our short résumé of the facts may have indicated, where much turned on the credibility of the evidence given by the appellant himself.

The judge's directions on this matter are in these terms:

> "It is my duty to say this to you: being of good character—by which we mean having no previous convictions and being highly thought of by his friends—can never be a defence to a criminal charge. We are, all of us, born into this world without previous convictions. Most of us hope to leave it in the same state. If, however, there is to be a conviction, there is going to be a first time. You can get somebody in that dock—and believe me, you do—with forty previous convictions. There was a time when that person did say to a judge and jury, 'I have no previous convictions.' So it can never be a defence to a criminal charge."

The learned judge should, in our judgment, have directed the jury that good character goes primarily to credibility, to whether the defendant should be believed by the jury or not. But it also has a further significance as explained in the decision

Printed in Dunstable, United Kingdom

67403478R00188